COMPUTERS
SIMPLIFIED

IDG's
IntroGraphic™ Series

by: maranGraphics' Development Group

IDG
BOOKS

IDG Books Worldwide, Inc.
An International Data Group Company

San Mateo, California ✦ Indianapolis, Indiana ✦ Boston, Massachusetts

Computers Simplified

Published by
IDG Books Worldwide, Inc.
An International Data Group Company
155 Bovet Road, Suite 310
San Mateo, CA 94402
(415) 312-0650

Copyright© 1994 by maranGraphics Inc.
5755 Coopers Avenue
Mississauga, Ontario, Canada
L4Z 1R9

Library of Congress Catalog Card No.: 94-079415
ISBN: 1-56884-651-7
Printed in the United States of America
10 9 8 7 6 5 4 3 2 1
Distributed in the United States by IDG Books Worldwide, Inc.

Distributed by Computer and Technical Books in Miami, Florida, for South America and the Caribbean; by Longman Singapore in Singapore, Malaysia, Thailand, and Korea; by Toppan Co. Ltd. in Japan; by Asia Computerworld in Hong Kong; by Woodslane Pty. Ltd. in Australia and New Zealand; and by Transworld Publishers Ltd. in the U.K. and Ireland.

For general information on IDG Books in the U.S., including information on discounts and premiums, contact IDG Books at 800-762-2974 or 317-895-5200.

For U.S. Corporate Sales and quantity discounts, contact maranGraphics at 800-469-6616, ext. 206.

For information on international sales of IDG Books, contact Christina Turner at 415-312-0633.

For information on translations, contact Marc Jeffrey Mikulich, Foreign Rights Manager, at IDG Books Worldwide. Fax Number 415-286-2747.

For sales inquiries and special prices for bulk quantities, write to the address above or call IDG Books Worldwide at 415-312-0650.

For information on using IDG Books in the classroom, or ordering examination copies, contact Jim Kelly at 800-434-2086.

Limits of Liability/Disclaimer of Warranty: The author and publisher of this book have used their best efforts in preparing this book. IDG Books Worldwide, Inc., International Data Group, Inc., and the author make no representation or warranties with respect to the accuracy or completeness of the contents of this book and specifically disclaim any implied warranties or merchantability or fitness for any particular purpose, and shall in no event be liable for any loss of profit or any other commercial damage, including but not limited to special, incidental, consequential, or other damages.

Trademark Acknowledgments

The animated characters are the copyright of maranGraphics, Inc.

U.S. Corporate Sales	**U.S. Trade Sales**
Contact maranGraphics at (800) 469-6616, ext. 206 or Fax (905) 890-9434.	Contact IDG Books at (800) 434-3422 or (415) 312-0650.

About IDG Books Worldwide

Welcome to the world of IDG Books Worldwide.

IDG Books Worldwide, Inc., is a subsidiary of International Data Group, the world's largest publisher of business and computer-related information and the leading global provider of information services on information technology. IDG was founded more than 25 years ago and now employs more than 5,700 people worldwide. IDG publishes more than 200 computer publications in 63 countries (see listing below). Forty million people read one or more IDG publications each month.

Launched in 1990, IDG Books is today the fastest-growing publisher of computer and business books in the United States. We are proud to have received 3 awards from the Computer Press Association in recognition of editorial excellence, and our best-selling ...For Dummies series has more than 10 million copies in print with translations in more than 20 languages. IDG Books, through a recent joint venture with IDG's Hi-Tech Beijing, became the first U.S. publisher to publish a computer book in the People's Republic of China. In record time, IDG Books has become the first choice for millions of readers around the world who want to learn how to better manage their businesses.

Our mission is simple: Every IDG book is designed to bring extra value and skill-building instructions to the reader. Our books are written by experts who understand and care about our readers. The knowledge base of our editorial staff comes from years of experience in publishing, education, and journalism — experience which we use to produce books for the '90s. In short, we care about books, so we attract the best people. We devote special attention to details such as audience, interior design, use of icons, and illustrations. And because we use an efficient process of authoring, editing, and desktop publishing our books electronically, we can spend more time ensuring superior content and spend less time on the technicalities of making books.

You can count on our commitment to deliver high-quality books at competitive prices on topics customers want to read about. At IDG, we value quality, and we have been delivering quality for more than 25 years. You'll find no better book on a subject than an IDG book.

John Kilcullen
President and CEO
IDG Books Worldwide, Inc.

IDG Books Worldwide, Inc., is a subsidiary of International Data Group. The officers are Patrick J. McGovern, Founder and Board Chairman; Walter Boyd, President. International Data Group's publications include: ARGENTINA'S Computerworld Argentina, Infoworld Argentina; AUSTRALIA'S Computerworld Australia, Australian PC World, Australian Macworld, Network World, Mobile Business Australia, Reseller, IDG Sources; AUSTRIA'S Computerwelt Oesterreich, PC Test; BRAZIL'S Computerworld, Gamepro, Game Power, Mundo IBM, Mundo Unix, PC World, Super Game; BELGIUM'S Data News (CW) BULGARIA'S Computerworld Bulgaria, Ediworld, PC & Mac World Bulgaria, Network World Bulgaria; CANADA'S CIO Canada, Computerworld Canada, Graduate Computerworld, InfoCanada, Network World Canada; CHILE'S Computerworld Chile, Informatica; COLOMBIA'S Computerworld Colombia, PC World; CZECH REPUBLIC'S Computerworld, Elektronika, PC World; DENMARK'S Communications World, Computerworld Danmark, Macintosh Produktkatalog, Macworld Danmark, PC World Danmark, PC World Produktguide, Tech World, Windows World; ECUADOR'S PC World Ecuador; EGYPT'S Computerworld (CW) Middle East, PC World Middle East; FINLAND'S MikroPC, Tietoviikko, Tietoverkko; FRANCE'S Distributique, GOLDEN MAC, InfoPC, Languages & Systems, Le Guide du Monde Informatique, Le Monde Informatique, Telecoms & Reseaux; GERMANY'S Computerwoche, Computerwoche Focus, Computerwoche Extra, Computerwoche Karriere, Information Management, Macwelt, Netzwelt, PC Welt, PC Woche, Publish, Unit; GREECE'S Infoworld, PC Games; HUNGARY'S Computerworld SZT, PC World; HONG KONG'S Computerworld Hong Kong, PC World Hong Kong; INDIA'S Computers & Communications; IRELAND'S ComputerScope; ISRAEL'S Computerworld Israel, PC World Israel; ITALY'S Computerworld Italia, Lotus Magazine, Macworld Italia, Networking Italia, PC Shopping, PC World Italia; JAPAN'S Computerworld Today, Information Systems World, Macworld Japan, Nikkei Personal Computing, SunWorld Japan, Windows World; KENYA'S East African Computer News; KOREA'S Computerworld Korea, Macworld Korea, PC World Korea; MEXICO'S Compu Edicion, Compu Manufactura, Computacion/Punto de Venta, Computerworld Mexico, MacWorld, Mundo Unix, PC World, Windows; THE NETHERLANDS' Computer! Totaal, Computable (CW), LAN Magazine, MacWorld, Totaal "Windows"; NEW ZEALAND'S Computer Listings, Computerworld New Zealand, New Zealand PC World, Network World; NIGERIA'S PC World Africa; NORWAY'S Computerworld Norge, C/World, Lotusworld Norge, Macworld Norge, Networld, PC World Ekspress, PC World Norge, PC World's Produktguide, Publish& Multimedia World, Student Data, Unix World, Windowsworld; IDG Direct Response; PAKISTAN'S PC World Pakistan; PANAMA'S PC World Panama; PERU'S Computerworld Peru, PC World; PEOPLE'S REPUBLIC OF CHINA'S China Computerworld, China Infoworld, Electronics Today/Multimedia World, Electronics International, Electronic Product World, China Network World, PC and Communications Magazine, PC World China, Software World Magazine, Telecom Product World; IDG HIGH TECH BEIJING'S New Product World; IDG SHENZHEN'S Computer News Digest; PHILIPPINES' Computerworld Philippines, PC Digest (PCW); POLAND'S Computerworld Poland, PC World/Komputer; PORTUGAL'S Cerebro/PC World, Correio Informatico/Computerworld, Informatica & Comunicacoes Catalogo, MacIn, Nacional de Produtos; ROMANIA'S Computerworld, PC World; RUSSIA'S Computerworld-Moscow, Mir - PC, Sety; SINGAPORE'S Computerworld Southeast Asia, PC World Singapore; SLOVENIA'S Monitor Magazine; SOUTH AFRICA'S Computer Mail (CIO) Computing S.A.,Network World S.A., Software World; SPAIN'S Advanced Systems, Amiga World, Computerworld Espana, Communicaciones World, Macworld Espana, NeXTWORLD, Super Juegos Magazine (GamePro), PC World Espana, Publish; SWEDEN'S Attack, ComputerSweden, Corporate Computing, Natverk & Kommunikation, Macworld, Mikrodatorn, PC World, Publishing & Design (CAP), Datalngenjoren, Maxi Data,Windows World; SWITZERLAND'S Computerworld Schweiz, Macworld Schweiz, PC Tip; TAIWAN'S Computerworld Taiwan, PC World Taiwan; THAILAND'S Thai Computerworld; TURKEY'S Computerworld Monitor, Macworld World Turkiye, PC World Turkiye; UKRAINE'S Computerworld; UNITED KINGDOM'S Computing /Computerworld, Connexion/Network World, Lotus Magazine, Macworld, Open Computing/Sunworld; UNITED STATES' Advanced Systems, AmigaWorld, Cable in the Classroom, CD Review, CIO, Computerworld, Digital Video, DOS Resource Guide, Electronic Entertainment Magazine, Federal Computer Week, Federal Integrator, GamePro, IDG Books, Infoworld, Infoworld Direct, Laser Event, Macworld, Multimedia World, Network World, PC Letter, PC World, PlayRight, Power PC World, Publish, SWATPro, Video Event; VENEZUELA'S Computerworld Venezuela, PC World; VIETNAM'S PC World Vietnam

Credits

Authors:
Richard Maran
Eric Feistmantl

Designer:
Jim C. Leung

Illustrator:
Dave Ross

Screen Artists:
Béla Korcsog
Dave Ross

Editors:
Gord Graham
Ruth Maran

Post Production:
Robert Maran

Acknowledgments

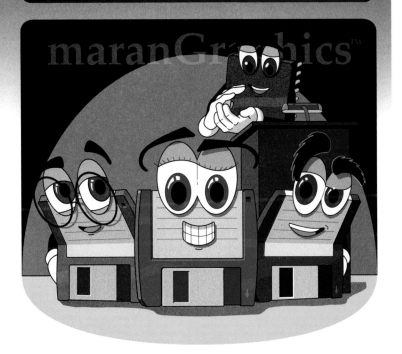

Our thanks to Tom Allan and Dave Semeniuk of IBM Canada. Their support and consultation was very much appreciated.

To the dedicated staff of maranGraphics, including David de Haas, Peters Ezers, David Hendricks, Jill Maran, Judy Maran, Maxine Maran, Robert Maran, Dave Ross, Christie Van Duin, Carol Walthers and Kelleigh Wing.

Special thanks to Karen Gillmore of the Francis Tuttle Vo-Tech Center for preparing the glossary section and her consultation on this project. And last, but not least, to Ruth Maran for writing the wordprocessing and spreadsheets chapters.

Table of Contents

HARDWARE AND SOFTWARE

What is Hardware?

"Hardware" is all the physical components of a computer system, such as the case and the monitor (screen). Any part of the computer that you can see or touch is considered hardware.

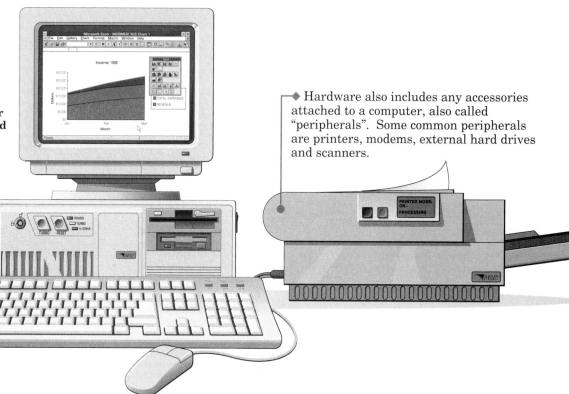

◆ Hardware also includes any accessories attached to a computer, also called "peripherals". Some common peripherals are printers, modems, external hard drives and scanners.

Understanding "Computerese"

Engineers and computer experts often use short forms known as "acronyms" for long words. Acronyms are created by using the first letter of a word or series of words.

ACRONYM	WHAT IT STANDS FOR	WHAT IT MEANS
MB	Megabyte	A measure of memory or storage. The more you have the better off you are.
MHz	Megahertz	A measure of processing speed. The higher the value, the faster a computer can work.
RAM	Random Access Memory	The electronic memory of a computer which is used to temporarily hold information. The more you have, the better.
SVGA	Super Video Graphics Array	The standard for a popular class of computer monitor.

◆ For most computer users "computerese" still sounds like a foreign language.

Try to remember what the acronym means instead of what each letter represents.

| GETTING STARTED | THE BASIC COMPUTER | INPUT/ OUTPUT | PROCESSING | STORAGE | PORTABLE COMPUTERS | OPERATING SYSTEMS | APPLICATION SOFTWARE | NETWORKING | GLOSSARY |

HARDWARE AND SOFTWARE
HOW COMPUTERS WORK

What is Software?

Software is a set of electronic instructions for the computer that helps you do something useful. Without software, computer hardware is like an airplane without a pilot.

You cannot actually see or touch software, although you can see the packages they come in. Two kinds of software exist: operating system software and application software.

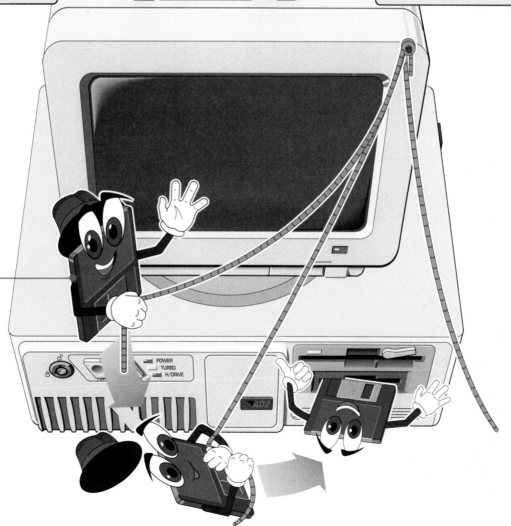

OPERATING SYSTEM SOFTWARE

This software sets the "rules" for how the computer, its peripherals (example: printer) and application programs, work together.

The most popular operating systems are MS-DOS, Windows and OS/2.

APPLICATION SOFTWARE

Application software enables you to write letters, analyze numbers, sort files, draw pictures and even play games.

Some popular applications include WordPerfect, Lotus 1-2-3 and dBASE.

◆ Software is usually loaded into the computer from diskettes.

Note: If a computer is part of a network, software can also be transferred to it through the network.

MicroFLOPPY
Double Sided

POWER
TURBO
H/DRIVE

HOW COMPUTERS WORK

How Computers Work

Computers process information using application software and instructions from the keyboard or mouse. The actual information processing occurs within the Central Processing Unit or CPU (the electronic brain). The results are sent to a monitor, printer, storage device or speaker.

INPUT

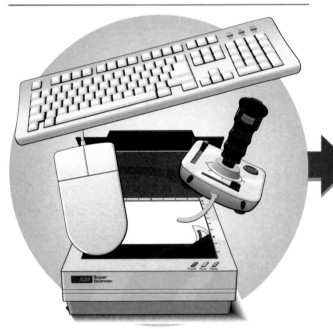

◆ Input devices act like the "eyes and ears" of the computer. They accept information and convert it into a format (or language) the CPU can work with.

Input devices include keyboards, mouse, joysticks and scanners.

PROCESSING

◆ The CPU uses the computer's electronic memory to help carry out instructions from the application software and accomplish a task (example: editing a letter, creating a graph, sorting numbers).

Sometimes information is saved to or retrieved from a storage device during processing.

| GETTING STARTED | THE BASIC COMPUTER | INPUT/ OUTPUT | PROCESSING | STORAGE | PORTABLE COMPUTERS | OPERATING SYSTEMS | APPLICATION SOFTWARE | NETWORKING | GLOSSARY |

HARDWARE AND SOFTWARE
HOW COMPUTERS WORK

OUTPUT

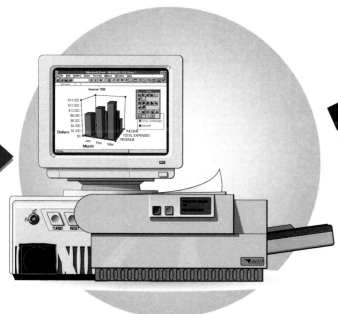

◆ Information processed by the CPU is sent to an output device or storage device. Output devices convert the computer language into a format we can work with, like a printout or a picture on a screen.

Output devices include monitors, printers and speakers.

STORAGE DEVICES

A storage device can act either as an input device or an output device.

◆ Information can be saved (output) to a storage device for future use. For example, a finished business letter can be saved to a hard drive.

◆ Information previously saved to a storage device can be retrieved (input) into the computer as required.

Storage devices include hard disk drives, floppy disk drives, tape backup units and CD-ROMs.

5

CASES

There are two main types of computer cases: desktop and tower. Your choice of case determines where it is best positioned in your work area, how much the computer can be expanded in the future and how easily it can be serviced.

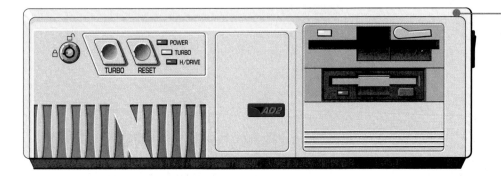

Desktop Case

Desktop computers have been around longer, are more popular and cost less than tower computers. They are the most popular choice for home and light-to-medium duty business applications.

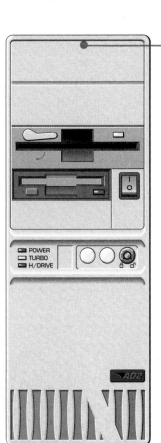

Tower Case

Tower computers are most often found in heavy-duty business settings. They can be expanded easily and offer excellent serviceability.

Full-sized tower units are placed on the floor rather than the desktop which can make floppy disk drives and other storage devices harder to reach.

TIP A "full-sized" tower or desktop case offers the widest range of upgrade options at the best cost. Smaller cases often use more expensive "non-standard" parts.

By staying with the standard full-sized cases, your future upgrade options are maximized while your costs are minimized.

| GETTING STARTED | THE BASIC COMPUTER | INPUT/ OUTPUT | PROCESSING | STORAGE | PORTABLE COMPUTERS | OPERATING SYSTEMS | APPLICATION SOFTWARE | NETWORKING | GLOSSARY |

CASES
EXPANSION CARDS
POWER SUPPLY

A Closer Look at a Desktop Computer Case

The case houses all the major components of the computer.

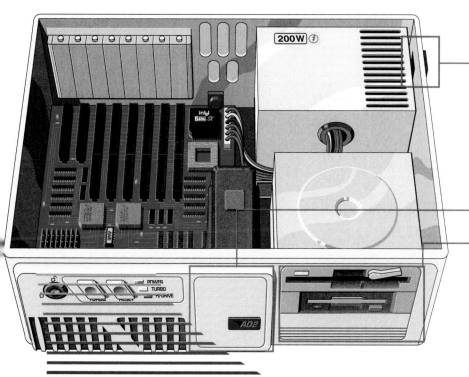

◆ **On/Off Switch**

◆ Hard disk drives are located behind this panel.

◆ Storage devices such as floppy disk drives, tape backup units or CD-ROM drives are located here.

These devices have openings to insert or remove diskettes, CD-ROMs or tape cassettes.

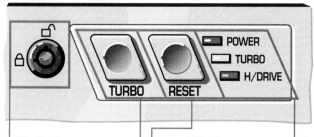

◆ **Keylock**

Locks the keyboard to prevent unauthorized access to the computer.

◆ **Reset Button**

Resets the computer should a "system crash" occur.

◆ **Turbo Button**

Switches the computer between two speeds. Normally, the computer operates at its fastest speed.

◆ **Status Indicators**

The green light is **on** when the computer is on.

The yellow light is **on** when the computer is operating at its fastest speed.

The red light is **on** when the hard disk is being used.

To get the best performance from your computer, make sure the turbo mode is **on**. Only a few, very old programs need to run at slower "non-turbo" speeds.

TIP

EXPANSION CARDS

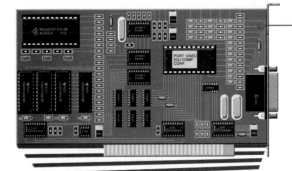

◆ **Expansion Card**

Want to add a nifty feature or two to your computer? If so, expansion cards are the answer! These cards are small circuit boards that can upgrade your computer to include:

▼ Enhanced graphics   ▼ Networking

▼ CD quality sound   ▼ Fax

▼ and many other functions

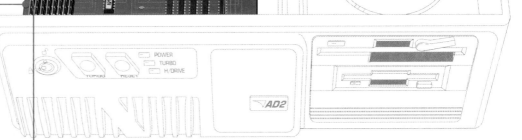

◆ **Motherboard**

Most of the basic components of the computer are built into the motherboard, a circuit board supplied with every computer.

◆ **Expansion Slots (also referred to as the "expansion bus")**

By installing expansion cards into expansion slots on the motherboard, a computer can be upgraded with new technologies as they become available.

Expansion slots provide an electrical "highway" to the CPU. The highway speed limit (or how fast information can move between the expansion card and the CPU) depends on the type of expansion slot you choose.

Note: Before you buy a computer, make sure its motherboard has enough empty expansion slots for your future needs.

GETTING STARTED	THE BASIC COMPUTER	INPUT/ OUTPUT	PROCESSING	STORAGE	PORTABLE COMPUTERS	OPERATING SYSTEMS	APPLICATION SOFTWARE	NETWORKING	GLOSSARY

CASES
EXPANSION CARDS
POWER SUPPLY

Types of Expansion Slots

ISA (Industry Standard Architecture)

"Popular and inexpensive" best defines the ISA standard.

Computers equipped with ISA expansion slots are fast enough for most home and office requirements.

ISA slots transfer data up to 16 megabytes/second.

OR

EISA (Enhanced Industry Standard Architecture)

"Powerful, fast and expensive". EISA systems are more popular with "power users" than home and business users.

Note: ISA cards can be used in an EISA slot, but without the speed and features of EISA.

EISA slots transfer data up to 32 megabytes/second.

OR

MCA (Micro Channel Architecture)

"Powerful, fast and expensive". Like EISA, MCA is better suited for computers running file servers or demanding applications.

MCA slots transfer data up to 40 megabytes/second.

LOCAL BUS SLOTS

Increasing demands on expansion cards such as video adapters can cause "bottlenecks" at the expansion slot. Local bus slots solve this problem by communicating at the maximum speed of the computer.

Local bus slots transfer data up to 130 megabytes/second.

TIPS

◆ ISA expansion slots come in two sizes. Cards that only fit in the longer slots (known as "16-bit cards") perform better than the shorter ones which fit either size (known as "8-bit cards").

◆ **The standard for local bus slots and cards is called "VL-Bus". Only buy a computer with local bus slots that matches this standard.**

Note: Some companies refer to "VL-BUS" as "VESA".

9

POWER SUPPLY

What is a Power Supply?

A power supply converts normal household electricity (AC) into electricity that can be used by the computer (DC). In addition, a fan inside the power supply keeps the air inside the computer case circulating, to prevent any internal components from overheating.

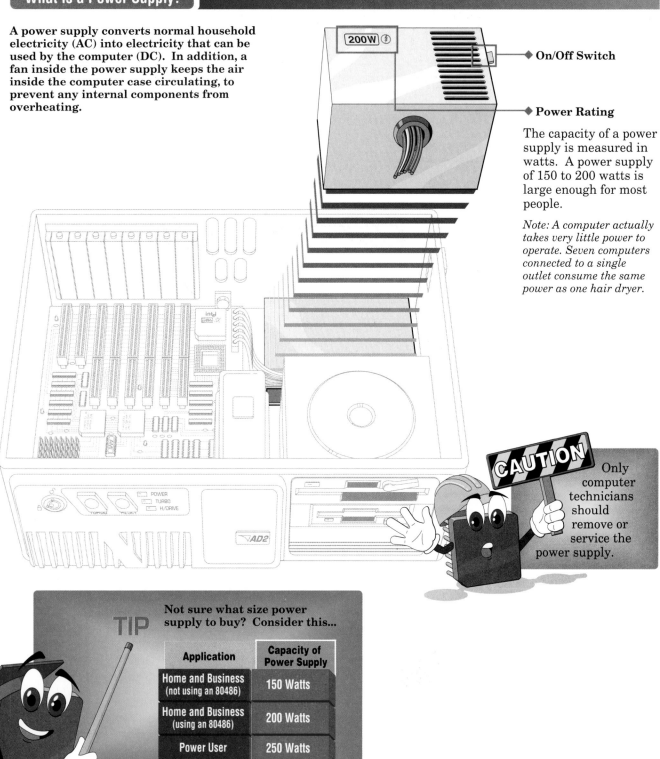

200W ⚡

◆ **On/Off Switch**

◆ **Power Rating**

The capacity of a power supply is measured in watts. A power supply of 150 to 200 watts is large enough for most people.

Note: A computer actually takes very little power to operate. Seven computers connected to a single outlet consume the same power as one hair dryer.

Only computer technicians should remove or service the power supply.

POWER
TURBO
H/DRIVE

AD2

TIP

Not sure what size power supply to buy? Consider this...

Application	Capacity of Power Supply
Home and Business (not using an 80486)	150 Watts
Home and Business (using an 80486)	200 Watts
Power User	250 Watts

CASES
EXPANSION CARDS
POWER SUPPLY

Protecting Your Equipment

Computers and peripherals such as printers should be unplugged during electrical storms, even if you have a surge suppressor. Telephone lines used for fax cards and modems should be unplugged as well.

First turn on the computer, monitor and printer. Then turn on any external modems, CD-ROM drives, tape backup units and other peripherals which use less power. This prevents "spikes" from "power-hungry hardware" damaging the smaller units. Follow the reverse to turn everything off.

POWER BARS

Power bars provide no protection against either large fluctuations of voltage known as "surges" or sudden short bursts of electricity known as "spikes". Their main function is to give you more power outlets.

SURGE AND SPIKE PROTECTOR

Surge and spike protectors provide "RFI/EMI filtering" to prevent computer damage from sudden fluctuations in voltage.

Note: These units do not protect computer systems against power failures.

UPS (Uninterruptible Power Supply)

The UPS contains a battery which stores electrical power. In the event of a power failure, the UPS uses the power stored in this battery to run the computer for a short time, so you can quickly save your file(s) and shut down your system.

KEYBOARD

The Parts of a Keyboard

◆ FUNCTION KEYS

Function keys are a quick way to give special commands within programs (example: pressing **F1** in a Windows application causes the help screen to appear).

Newer keyboards have 12 function keys across the top, while older keyboards have 10 function keys along the left.

◆ ESCAPE KEY

In many programs, the **Esc** key returns you to the previous menu screen or exits from the program.

◆ CONTROL AND ALTERNATE KEYS

Using the **Ctrl** and/or **Alt** keys in combination with other keys offer additional choices. (example: pressing **Alt** and **F4** at the same time exits from Windows).

◆ Many keyboards have small "bumps" on the **D** and **K** or the **F** and **J** keys. These bumps help touch-typists quickly position their fingers on the keyboard without looking.

TWO TYPES OF KEYBOARDS

◆ "Soft touch" keyboards use "mushy" feeling keys that are almost silent when you press them.

◆ Regular keyboards "click" when you press them.

◆ The type of keyboard you select depends entirely on your preference.

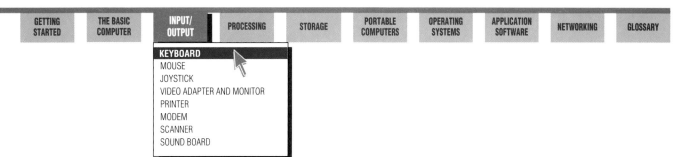

KEYBOARD
MOUSE
JOYSTICK
VIDEO ADAPTER AND MONITOR
PRINTER
MODEM
SCANNER
SOUND BOARD

◆ BACKSPACE KEY

Erases the characters before the cursor, one at a time.

◆ TEXT EDITING

Used mostly in word processing programs, the text editing keys are used to quickly move around a document and control how text is inserted into it.

◆ LED STATUS INDICATORS

These lights are "lit" when special keyboard switches are turned on (example: when you press Caps Lock, the **Caps Lock** light comes on, and any character you type appears as a capital letter "abcd"="ABCD").

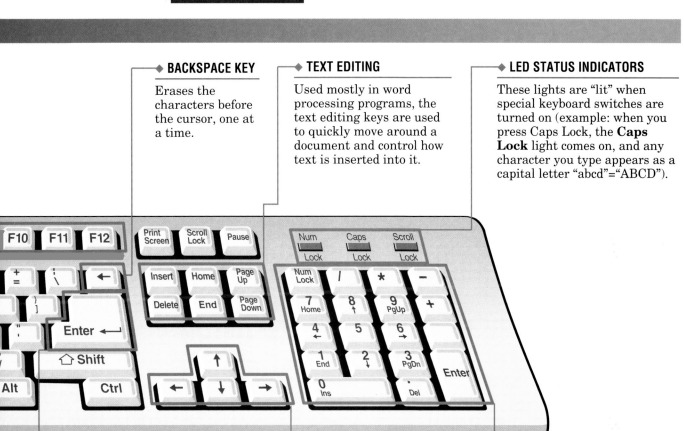

◆ ENTER KEY

In the operating system, pressing **Enter** starts a command (example: typing **dir** in MS-DOS, and then pressing **Enter** displays all the files in the current directory).

In word processing programs, pressing **Enter** starts a new paragraph.

In spreadsheet or database programs, pressing **Enter** inputs a value or gives a command.

◆ CURSOR KEYS

Used for moving the cursor around the screen. The cursor indicates where text or graphics will be inserted or erased on the screen.

Note: The mouse has replaced the cursor keys in many applications.

◆ NUMERIC KEYPAD/ CURSOR KEYS

Provides a quick and convenient way of entering long lists of numbers. Also used as cursor keys (on keyboards without a separate set of cursor keys) for moving around the computer screen.

◆ If you hold down a key, it will automatically begin to repeat.

TIP

Example: hold down the **D** key and it will repeat itself on the screen until you release the key.

MOUSE

What is a Mouse?

Many programs sold today are designed to work with a mouse. For operating systems such as Windows and OS/2, a mouse is essential. A mouse is used to replace hard-to-learn key combinations with easier "point and click" actions.

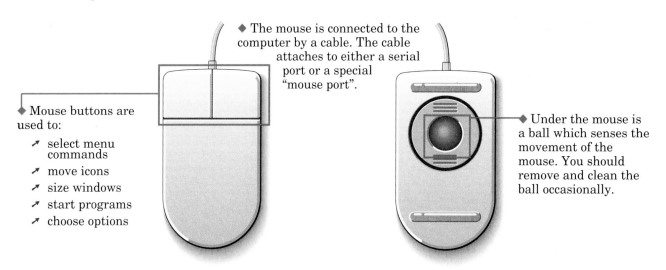

◆ The mouse is connected to the computer by a cable. The cable attaches to either a serial port or a special "mouse port".

◆ Mouse buttons are used to:

- ➚ select menu commands
- ➚ move icons
- ➚ size windows
- ➚ start programs
- ➚ choose options

◆ Under the mouse is a ball which senses the movement of the mouse. You should remove and clean the ball occasionally.

Holding the Mouse

◆ Hold the mouse as shown in the diagram. This way the thumb and the rightmost two fingers can guide the mouse while the remaining two fingers can press the mouse buttons.

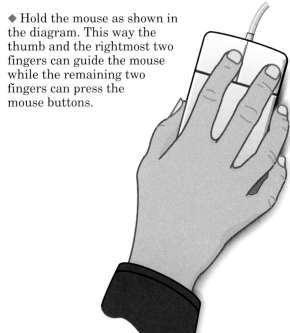

LEFT-HANDED USERS

The mouse buttons can be "reversed" in any Windows or OS/2 application for use by left-handed people. Consult your manual for further instructions.

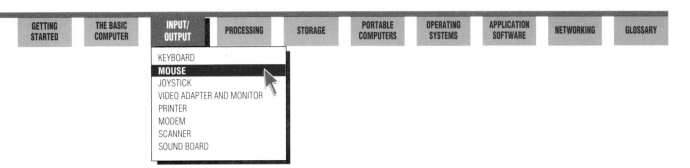

Using the Mouse

MOUSE POINTER

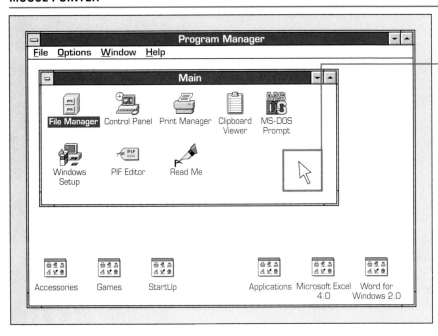

◆ A pointer on the screen represents the mouse. Moving the mouse moves the pointer on the screen.

In MS-DOS, the pointer is often a flashing line ▬. Windows and OS/2 often use a pointer in the shape of an arrow slanted to one side ▷.

◆ The shape of the mouse pointer can change to indicate different capabilities. For example, the mouse pointer may change to I when the program is ready to be used for editing.

MOVING THE MOUSE POINTER

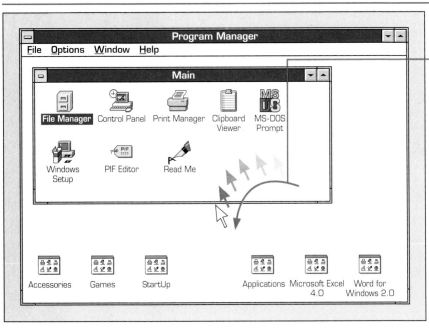

◆ The pointer moves as you move the mouse (example: the pointer moves down as you move the mouse down).

15

Do I Need a Mouse?

Operating System	Mouse required
MS-DOS	No
WINDOWS	Yes
OS/2	Yes

◆ But many MS-DOS applications support a mouse. Consult your manual for further information.

Common Mouse Terms

TERM	WHAT IT MEANS
Point	Move the pointer on the screen until it is over the desired location.
Click	Quickly press and release the left mouse button.
Double-Click	Quickly press the left mouse button twice.
Drag	Hold down the left mouse button while moving the mouse.
Drag and Drop	Hold down the left mouse button while moving the mouse. Release the mouse button when the pointer is over the desired location.

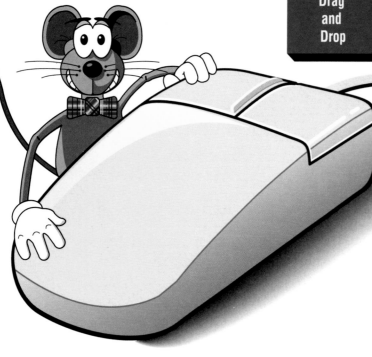

TIPS

◆ A mouse requires a "software driver" to operate. Check that a driver for your operating system or application program is included before purchasing a mouse.

◆ If after extended use the mouse pointer does not move smoothly try cleaning your mouse. Consult your mouse manual for instructions.

KEYBOARD
MOUSE
JOYSTICK
VIDEO ADAPTER AND MONITOR
PRINTER
MODEM
SCANNER
SOUND BOARD

What is a Joystick?

A joystick is a pointing device commonly used in games. It provides more realistic control for many games (example: flight simulators) than a keyboard or mouse.

Note: Joysticks are not used for business applications such as word processing, spreadsheets or databases.

◆ A joystick continuously sends signals to the computer telling it the current position of the handle. The program uses this information to update its actions.

For example, a "jet" in a flight simulator would dive according to how far the joystick (flight stick) is pushed forward.

◆ Most joysticks come with one or two buttons used for special functions (example: to fire a missile or activate a menu).

◆ Joysticks attach to the computer using a cable connected to a "game port". Most computers come with one game port.

◆ Small sliders known as "trim controls" are used to adjust the joystick for different computers. This is often done by centering a cross hair on the screen.

VIDEO ADAPTER AND MONITOR

How Graphics are Displayed

Computer information is displayed visually with a video adapter card and monitor.

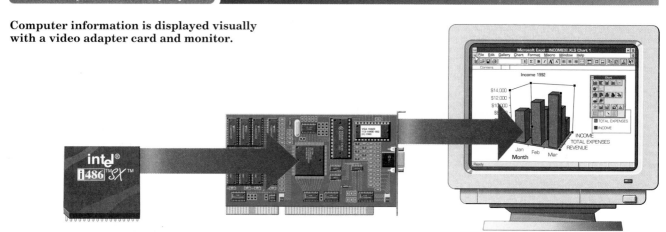

◆ Information processed within the CPU that needs to be visually displayed is sent to the video adapter.

◆ The video adapter converts information from the format used by the CPU into a format used by the monitor.

◆ The monitor displays information sent to it by the video adapter much as a television displays information sent to it by a cable service.

What is a Video Adapter?

A video adapter converts information from the CPU into a format used by the monitor. It is as though the CPU only speaks Russian, while the monitor only understands English. The video adapter's job is to translate Russian into English.

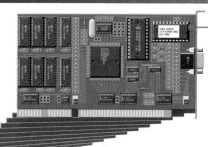

◆ The video adapter can be built into the motherboard, but in most cases it is installed as an expansion card.

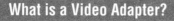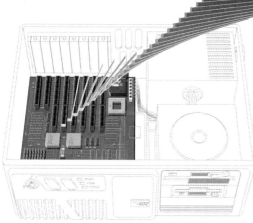

The resolution, the number of on-screen colors and the speed at which graphics appear on the screen are all determined by the combination of video adapter and monitor you use.

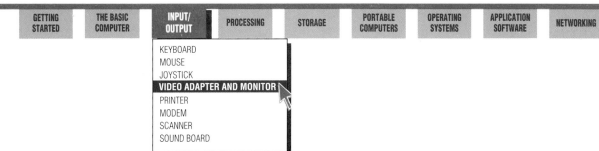

Resolution

Resolution is the total number of horizontal and vertical pixels that a monitor can display. A pixel is the smallest dot the computer can control on the screen.

The more pixels the computer can control, the higher the resolution and the more detail the monitor can display.

Note: Pixel stands for "Picture Element".

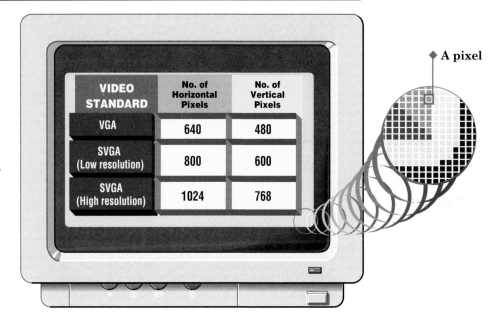

◆ A pixel

VIDEO STANDARD	No. of Horizontal Pixels	No. of Vertical Pixels
VGA	640	480
SVGA (Low resolution)	800	600
SVGA (High resolution)	1024	768

Video Standards

At present, there are two main standards for video adapters and monitors. These standards ensure that your video card and monitor will be compatible with all popular programs and operating systems.

◆ VGA (Video Graphics Array) is suited for low-budget home and business applications.

◆ SVGA (pronounced Super VGA) has greater detail and truer colors than VGA. With a resolution of 800x600, SVGA is ideal for business applications.

◆ SVGA, with a resolution of 1024x768 is ideal for more graphic-intensive applications (example: desktop publishing, CAD/CAM).

19

VIDEO ADAPTER AND MONITOR

Color

Depending on your application, you can select a system that displays a certain number of colors on your monitor.

Number of Colors	Sometimes called...	Recommended For		
		MS-DOS Applications	Windows, OS/2 Applications	Professional Use
16	4-bit color	✓		
256	8-bit color		✓	
16.7 million	24-bit color			✓

◆ Required for applications such as CAD/CAM or color desktop publishing.

Note: How much information the video adapter must process is directly proportional to the number of colors and resolution you need.

Only the fastest video adapters will yield acceptable performance when displaying 16.7 million colors at high resolution.

Memory

Video adapters contain their own memory, separate from the computer's built-in memory. The amount of memory installed on the video adapter card determines the maximum number of colors that can be displayed at a given resolution.

Entry-level cards often come with 256K.

Video cards used with Windows or OS/2 should have at least 1MB.

Note: For a description of memory, refer to pages 36 through 39.

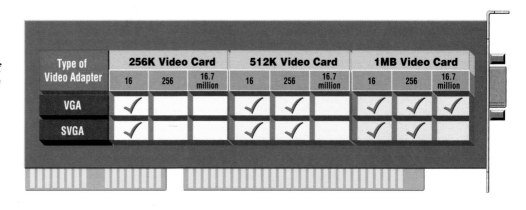

Type of Video Adapter	256K Video Card			512K Video Card			1MB Video Card		
	16	256	16.7 million	16	256	16.7 million	16	256	16.7 million
VGA	✓			✓	✓		✓	✓	✓
SVGA	✓			✓	✓		✓	✓	

KEYBOARD
MOUSE
JOYSTICK
VIDEO ADAPTER AND MONITOR
PRINTER
MODEM
SCANNER
SOUND BOARD

Performance of Video Adapters

TYPES OF MEMORY CHIPS

Two types of memory chips are used in video adapters:

◆ RAM chips are inexpensive but slow. They are used in "entry-level" video adapters and MS-DOS applications.

◆ VRAM (VideoRAM) chips run twice as fast as RAM chips but cost more. Use video adapters with VRAM chips for Windows and OS/2 applications.

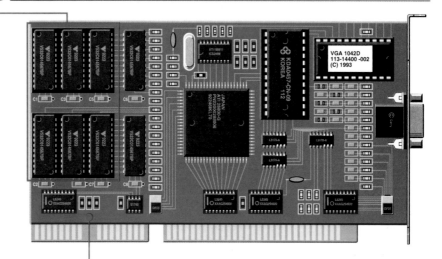

TYPES OF VIDEO ADAPTERS

Frame Buffer

◆ Screen images are generated by the CPU and sent to the video adapter. The memory in the video adapter (the Frame Buffer) holds the image until it is changed. Small changes to the image require only small changes to the memory and can be done quickly. Large changes (example: when a page is scrolled off screen) take time, as the entire contents of the memory must be redrawn.

◆ Frame buffer video cards perform best with computers equipped with a fast CPU and expansion bus.

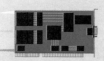

Accelerator

◆ Screen images are generated by a processor located on the video adapter. Since the processor works in conjunction with the CPU, screen updates are up to 24 times faster than with a frame buffer.

Accelerators require "software drivers". While only one driver is required for Windows or OS/2, a different software driver is required for each MS-DOS application.

◆ Accelerator performance depends on the quality of software drivers you use. For best performance always use the most up-to-date software drivers.

21

VIDEO ADAPTER AND MONITOR

Monitor

You communicate visually with the computer through the monitor. The better the quality of the screen, the longer you can look at it before your eyes get tired.

◆ **Anti-Glare**

Some monitors have etched or coated glass to reduce reflections. Reflections from light sources such as overhead lighting can make viewing the screen difficult.

Note: External "anti-glare" screens can be added to monitors without etched or coated glass.

◆ **Dot Pitch**

Dot Pitch measures the size of the holes on the screen. As with a flour sifter, the finer the screen the better the quality. The smaller the dot pitch, the "finer" the detail displayed.

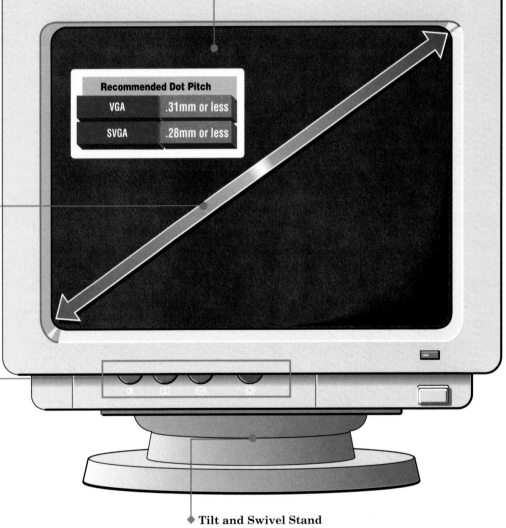

Recommended Dot Pitch	
VGA	.31mm or less
SVGA	.28mm or less

◆ **Size**

Size is measured in inches diagonally across the screen.

◆ **Controls**

Various controls are placed on the monitor (example: brightness, contrast). On better monitors, these controls are grouped together, easy to reach and clearly labeled.

◆ **Tilt and Swivel Stand**

Some monitors have stands which can be "tilted and swiveled" to make viewing easier.

KEYBOARD
MOUSE
JOYSTICK
VIDEO ADAPTER AND MONITOR
PRINTER
MODEM
SCANNER
SOUND BOARD

Quick Selection Guide

HOME

 **Video Adapter**

- Frame Buffer
- VRAM Memory
- VGA, 512K

 Monitor

- 14"
- .31mm (Dot Pitch)

BUSINESS

 **Video Adapter**

- Accelerator
- VRAM Memory
- SVGA, 1MB

 Monitor

- 14" or 15"
- .28mm (Dot Pitch)

DESKTOP PUBLISHING

 **Video Adapter**

- Accelerator
- VRAM Memory
- SVGA, 4MB

 Monitor

- 17", 19" or 21"
- .28mm or less (Dot Pitch)

◆ When the same image is displayed on a monitor for a long time, it leaves a "shadow" or "screen burn". To prevent screen burn, use a "screen-saver" program that blanks out the monitor when you're not using it.

Note: Windows and OS/2 include built-in screen savers.

◆ Some monitors "flicker" at high resolutions. This is because the video adapter and monitor **TIPS** are using a cost-cutting technique known as "interlacing". Always try out the equipment before you purchase it and specify a "non-interlaced" system.

◆ If you plan to use a variety of graphics' standards, consider purchasing a "multisync monitor". These monitors can automatically adapt to new graphics' standards.

PRINTER

What is a Printer?

After a document is created on the computer, you can send it to a printer for a "hard copy" (printout).

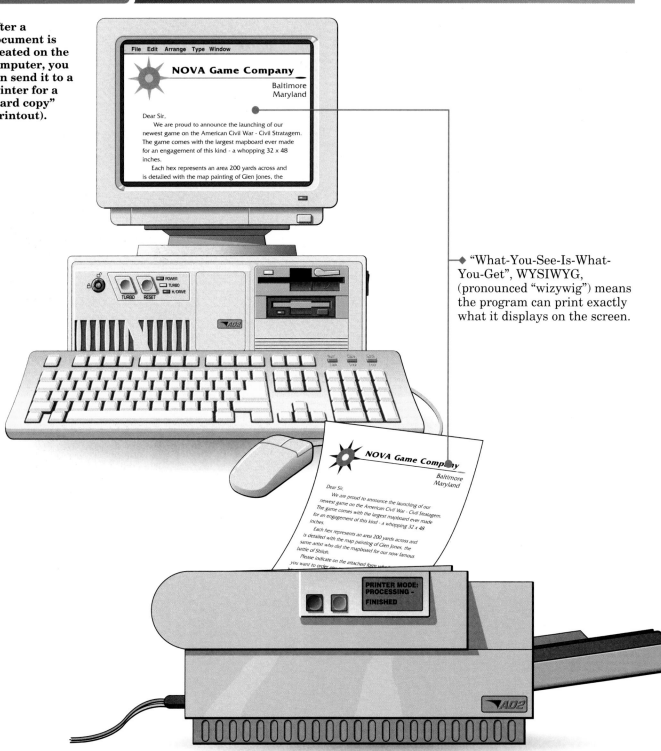

♦ "What-You-See-Is-What-You-Get", WYSIWYG, (pronounced "wizywig") means the program can print exactly what it displays on the screen.

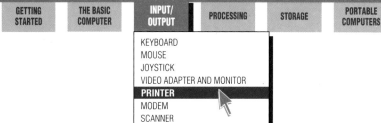

| GETTING STARTED | THE BASIC COMPUTER | INPUT/ OUTPUT | PROCESSING | STORAGE | PORTABLE COMPUTERS | OPERATING SYSTEMS | APPLICATION SOFTWARE | NETWORKING | GLOSSARY |

KEYBOARD
MOUSE
JOYSTICK
VIDEO ADAPTER AND MONITOR
PRINTER
MODEM
SCANNER
SOUND BOARD

Choosing a Printer

SPEED OF THE PRINTER

Printers are rated either by "pages per minute" (PPM) or by "characters per second" (CPS).

The higher the value, the faster the speed, although the complexity of the page is a major factor (example: if graphics are included).

QUALITY OF THE OUTPUT

The quality of a printout is measured in "dots per inch" or dpi. The more dots per inch, the more detailed the output.

Generally, 300 dpi is acceptable for office applications.

TIP

If a more detailed output is required, you can send the file to a "service bureau" for output at resolutions of 1270, 2540 or 3386 dpi.

SPECIAL FEATURES

◆ Some printers offer special features such as color and large page formats.

◆ Check with your dealer or computer expert if you require any special features.

SOFTWARE SUPPORT

The software which controls the printer is known as a "printer driver".

Always check the printer drivers in your programs and operating system to see if they support the printer you plan to use.

Laser Printers

Laser printers work a lot like photocopiers, but rather than supplying a "real" page to be copied, the computer sends the laser printer a "digital" page in electronic form.

◆ Most laser printers are rated in "pages per minute". Most printers output 4 to 8 pages per minute, while faster printers can produce 12 pages per minute or more.

◆ Laser printers, like photocopiers, have trays to hold blank paper to print on. Printers with larger trays (example: 500 pages) are better suited for busier office environments.

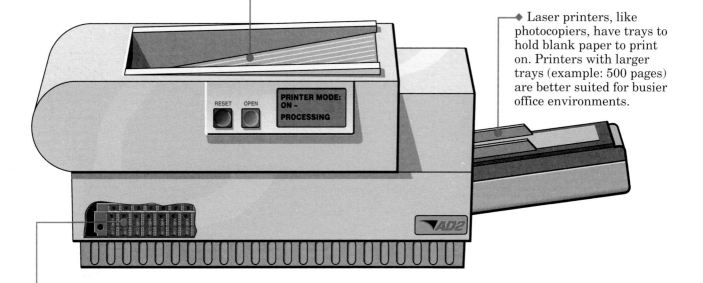

RESET   OPEN   PRINTER MODE:
ON –
PROCESSING

AD2

◆ Like computers, printers contain electronic memory. The amount of memory determines how complex a page the printer can output.

Laser printers should have a minimum of 2MB of memory, although 4MB is recommended. If a printer appears to be "processing" a page and then suddenly quits, it probably requires more memory.

TYPES OF LASER PRINTERS

PRINTER CONTROL LANGUAGE

◆ Printer Control Language (PCL) printers have similar resolutions and speeds as PostScript printers but cost much less. PCL-based printers can handle average office tasks.

POSTSCRIPT

◆ PostScript printers cost more than PCL printers and are designed for graphics work. A major advantage of PostScript is its widespread acceptance throughout the graphic arts industry.

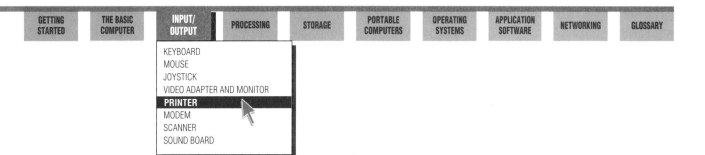

| GETTING STARTED | THE BASIC COMPUTER | INPUT/ OUTPUT | PROCESSING | STORAGE | PORTABLE COMPUTERS | OPERATING SYSTEMS | APPLICATION SOFTWARE | NETWORKING | GLOSSARY |

KEYBOARD
MOUSE
JOYSTICK
VIDEO ADAPTER AND MONITOR
PRINTER
MODEM
SCANNER
SOUND BOARD

Dot-Matrix Printer

In a dot-matrix printer the print-head physically "hits" the paper through the ribbon. Dot-matrix printers can produce printouts on "multi-part" forms because they work by impact.

Although dot-matrix printers are inexpensive, they are louder, slower and produce lower print quality than laser printers.

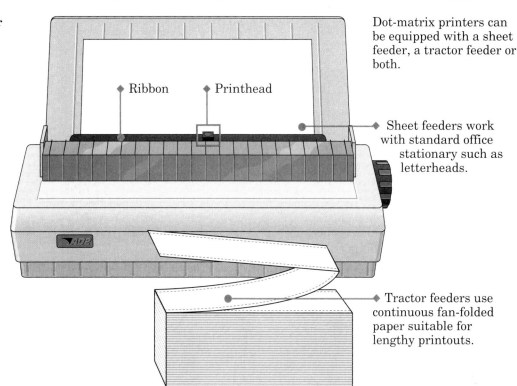

◆ Ribbon   ◆ Printhead

Dot-matrix printers can be equipped with a sheet feeder, a tractor feeder or both.

◆ Sheet feeders work with standard office stationary such as letterheads.

◆ Tractor feeders use continuous fan-folded paper suitable for lengthy printouts.

PRINTER RECOMMENDATIONS

◆ Unless you need to use multi-part forms or continuous fan-folded paper, buy the fastest laser printer you can afford. They are faster, quieter and produce better type and graphics than dot-matrix printers.

◆ PCL laser printers are best-suited for general office correspondence while PostScript laser printers are best suited for graphics work.

◆ Dot-matrix printers are inexpensive and the only choice if you need to use continuous fan-folded paper.

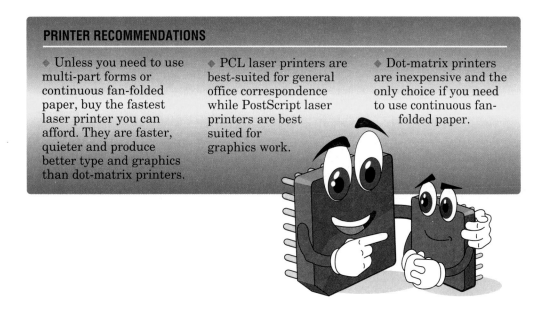

MODEM

What is a Modem?

A modem enables your computer to "talk on the phone" with another computer, if each has a compatible modem.

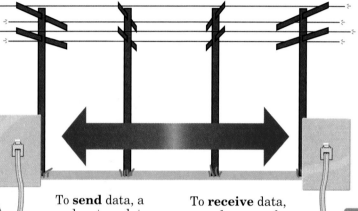

To **send** data, a modem translates the format a computer uses to a format the telephone line transmits.

To **receive** data, a modem translates the data from the telephone line back to a format the computer understands.

What are Modems used for?

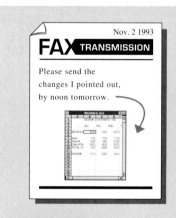

ON-LINE SERVICES

On-line services offer a diverse range of features such as electronic mail, shopping at home, banking and travel reservations.

Popular on-line services include CompuServe, GEnie, and America Online.

FILE TRANSFERS

Modems allow programs and data to be transmitted locally or around the world through phone lines.

Example: To send a file to a person at another location, you could either mail a diskette, or send it by modem.

FAX SERVICES

Some modems include software that allows documents (files) created on your computer to be sent to remote fax machines.

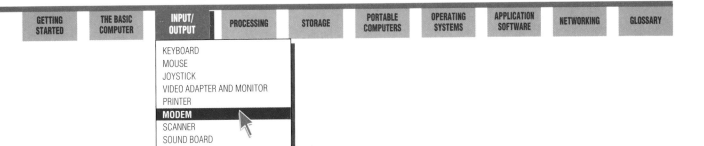

| GETTING STARTED | THE BASIC COMPUTER | INPUT/ OUTPUT | PROCESSING | STORAGE | PORTABLE COMPUTERS | OPERATING SYSTEMS | APPLICATION SOFTWARE | NETWORKING | GLOSSARY |

KEYBOARD
MOUSE
JOYSTICK
VIDEO ADAPTER AND MONITOR
PRINTER
MODEM
SCANNER
SOUND BOARD

External Modem

You control a modem using a communications program. Always make sure the modem is turned on before starting your communications program.

◆ When the modem is first turned on, various options are set according to the positions of various tiny "DIP switches".

◆ A special cable, known as a serial cable, connects the modem to the computer's serial port.

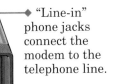

◆ "Line-in" phone jacks connect the modem to the telephone line.

◆ Some modems have "line-out" phone jacks enabling you to use the same telephone line for other purposes.

◆ Status lights

◆ Power switch

◆ Power cord

Internal Modem

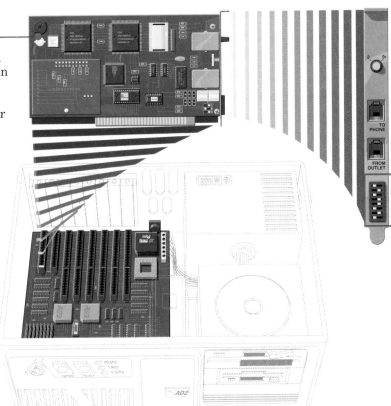

◆ Installed in an expansion slot, an internal modem operates off the computer's power supply, so it is always on.

◆ Internal modems have a volume control, DIP switches and one or two phone jacks on the back of the expansion card (at the rear of the computer).

These controls work the same as those on an external modem.

MODEM

Speed

The speed of a modem is measured in bits per second (bps). The higher the "bps", the faster data can be transmitted between computers.

Business

◆ For business applications, 14,400 bps modems are the best choice.

Home

◆ For home applications, 2400 bps modems are a good, inexpensive choice.

If you find "bits/sec" (bps) difficult to understand, converting to "characters/sec" (cps) or "words/sec" (wps) may be easier. Take the "bps" value and divide by 10 for characters/sec, or by 60 for words/sec.

TIP

Characters/sec
2400 bps / 10 = 240 cps

Words/sec
2400 bps / 60 = 40 wps

MODEM STANDARDS

There are three modem standards: V.22bis, V.32 and V.32bis.

Each modem standard has a maximum speed for transferring information.

Modem Standard	Maximum Speed (bps)	Fall-Back Speed (bps)				Fall-Forward
		12000	9600	7200	4800	
V.22bis	2400					
V.32	9600				✓	
V.32bis	14400	✓	✓	✓	✓	✓

◆ Faster transfer speeds require telephone lines which are "noise" free. On noisy telephone lines, the modem "falls-back" to a slower transfer speed.

Note: The modem "falls-back" to the fastest transfer speed that the telephone line and modem standard allow.

◆ If the telephone line quality improves during transmission, a "V.32bis" modem "falls-forward" or advances to the fastest speed the telephone line permits.

KEYBOARD
MOUSE
JOYSTICK
VIDEO ADAPTER AND MONITOR
PRINTER
MODEM
SCANNER
SOUND BOARD

Compression

Computer information (example: data and programs) can be compressed (reduced) in size to increase the transmission speed.

◆ Many modems have built-in "compression" programs which squeeze down the information being sent and return it to its original state when received.

Compression Standard	Performance Enhancement
MNP 5	2X
CCITT V.42bis	4X

Note: Both the receiving and sending modems must use the same compression programs (example: MNP 5 or CCITT V.42bis) for the compression to work.

◆ Since compressed information uses 50% to 75% less space, transmitting compressed information takes 50% to 75% less time.

SCANNER

A scanner is a peripheral used for input.

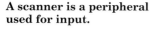

Under the control of computer software, a scanner translates what it "sees" on a page into a format the computer can use. This process is known as "digitizing" or "scanning". A scanner is like an office copier, except it creates a file instead of a paper copy.

The scanned object can be displayed on a monitor, edited, stored or sent to a printer.

What are Scanners used for?

ILLUSTRATIONS

Diagrams and sketches can be digitized and then imported into a desktop publishing program. For example, a map can be quickly scanned into the computer and then used in a newsletter.

ARCHIVES

Catalogues can quickly be digitized and stored in a computer for future reference. Compared to paper, information stored in a computer is easier to retrieve, takes up less room and lasts indefinitely.

OPTICAL CHARACTER RECOGNITION (OCR)

Using special software, many scanners can "read" text. This process is known as "**O**ptical **C**haracter **R**ecognition" or **OCR**. Pages of text can be quickly scanned in faster than typing them.

KEYBOARD
MOUSE
JOYSTICK
VIDEO ADAPTER AND MONITOR
PRINTER
MODEM
SCANNER
SOUND BOARD

How to Choose a Scanner

RESOLUTION

The level of detail a scanner can resolve is measured in dots per inch, or dpi. Most scanners can work at 300 dpi or higher.

Increasing the dpi improves the quality of the scan but produces a larger file. It takes more computer resources (example: hard drive space and RAM memory) to process the larger files.

LINE ART

Many scanners have a special setting known as "line-art mode" used to scan black and white drawings. Line-art scans require less system resources (example: hard drive space and RAM memory) than gray-scale or color scans.

GRAY-SCALE

The number of shades of gray the scanner can distinguish is called the "gray-scale". Most scanners can distinguish up to 256 shades of gray (called 8-bit). Increasing the number of gray-scales creates a scan which is more accurate but requires more system resources.

Number of Gray-scales	Commonly Called	Examples
1	Line Art Mode	
4	2-bit	
16	4-bit	
256	8-bit	

COLOR

A color scanner senses shades of red, blue and green. Many color scanners can differentiate between 16.7 million colors (also called "true-color" or "24-bit color"). True-color images require a considerable amount of system resources.

Note: Some scanners scan images in modes other than "true-color" (example: 256 color). These scanned images will not appear as lifelike, but require less system resources.

◆ When purchasing a scanner, make sure the software included with the package works with your operating system (example: Windows 3.1). **TIPS**

◆ To edit scanned images, your computer should be equipped with a 1MB SVGA video adapter.

SOUND BOARD

What is a Sound Board?

Sound boards allow a computer to output high-quality sound and music. Some boards include the ability to talk (speech-synthesis) and record sounds.

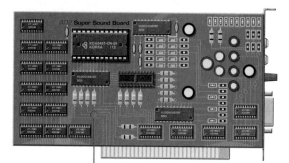

◆ Sound boards are installed inside the computer as an expansion card.

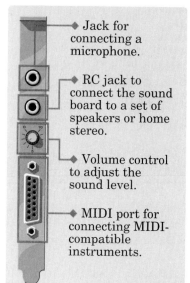

◆ Jack for connecting a microphone.

◆ RC jack to connect the sound board to a set of speakers or home stereo.

◆ Volume control to adjust the sound level.

◆ MIDI port for connecting MIDI-compatible instruments.

◆ Sound boards are recommended for games and multimedia applications. **TIP**

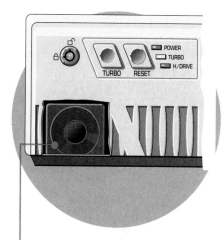

◆ Sound boards replace the simple "beeps" generated by the computer's internal speaker, with high-quality sound and music.

◆ Many sound boards generate enough power to run small speakers. If you prefer window-shaking sound you can use the RC jack to connect the sound board to your home stereo.

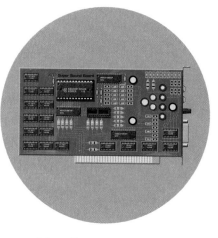

◆ Not all sound boards can produce stereo sound. For best sound reproduction, always ask the dealer if a sound board is "stereo" before you buy it.

KEYBOARD
MOUSE
JOYSTICK
VIDEO ADAPTER AND MONITOR
PRINTER
MODEM
SCANNER
SOUND BOARD

What are Sound Boards used for?

◆ Digitized sound effects, musical soundtracks and speech add to the excitement and realism of games. For example, flying a jet is more exciting when you can hear the "roar" of its engines.

◆ Operating systems that support sound boards (example: Windows) can have sound effects added to ordinary tasks. A "broken glass" sound can indicate an incorrect choice.

◆ Voice messages can be recorded and used in certain computer applications. Clicking the mouse on a "note icon" can start a recorded voice message.

Note: Not all sound boards can record sounds or voice messages. Check for this option before purchasing a sound board.

What is MIDI?

MIDI (Musical Instrument Digital Interface) is a standard that enables you to connect your computer to a wide variety of musical synthesizers and instruments.

The computer can be used to create, edit, store and playback music.

◆ A wide variety of instruments can be connected to the computer (example: keyboards). Many musicians use MIDI instruments to create and edit their recordings.

MEMORY

◆ **Electronic Memory**

Electronic Memory, often called "RAM" (Random Access Memory) stores information temporarily. If the power is interrupted, even for an instant, this information is lost forever.

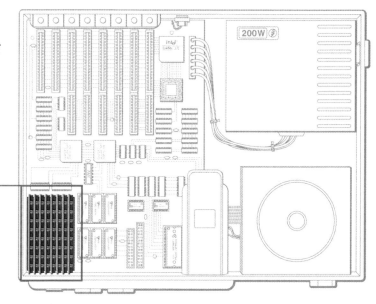

How Memory Works

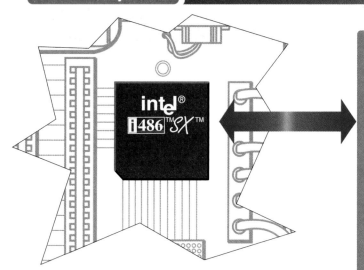

The central processing unit (CPU) is the electronic brain of the computer.

The CPU accesses information from electronic memory (RAM) as required, processes it, and then returns it to RAM.

ELECTRONIC MEMORY (RAM)

Electronic memory is like your desk, the bigger it is, the more documents you can spread out at once. Similarly, the more RAM in your computer, the more information your computer can work with.

Electronic memory is used to store data and instructions from the operating system and any application programs you are using. It works like an electronic blackboard that is constantly written, erased and rewritten.

Data and instructions are stored in RAM as individual characters (also called bytes). A byte can represent any character (example: a, b, A, B, 1, 2, 3, ?, #, !).

| GETTING STARTED | THE BASIC COMPUTER | INPUT/ OUTPUT | PROCESSING | STORAGE | PORTABLE COMPUTERS | OPERATING SYSTEMS | APPLICATION SOFTWARE | NETWORKING | GLOSSARY |

MEMORY
CENTRAL PROCESSING UNIT

Measuring Memory

TERM	WHAT IT MEANS
Byte	One character
Kilo	Metric for "one thousand"
Mega	Metric for "one million"
Giga	Metric for "one billion"
Kilobyte (K)	One thousand characters
Megabyte (MB)	One million characters
Gigabyte (GB)	One billion characters

◆ *Note: Kilobytes, Megabytes and Gigabytes are used to measure the size of electronic (temporary) memory and storage devices (permanent memory).*

The values of Kilobytes, Megabytes and Gigabytes are normally rounded off for convenience.

Example: 1 Kilobyte is actually 2^{10} or 1,024 bytes.

Therefore:

640 Kilobytes = 640 x 1,024 = 655,360 bytes

not 640 x 1,000 = 640,000 bytes

TIP

◆ **Is your disk activity light always "on" ?**

◆ **Does the computer suddenly run slower when running more than one application in Windows or OS/2?**

◆ **Does a program loading from the hard drive suddenly quit?**

SOLUTION:

Ask your computer technician to add more memory (RAM) to your computer.

How much Memory does my Computer have?

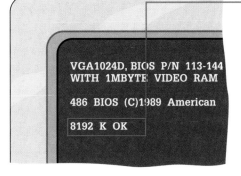

VGA1024D, BIOS P/N 113-144
WITH 1MBYTE VIDEO RAM

486 BIOS (C)1989 American

8192 K OK

◆ When a computer is first turned on, it checks to see if its memory is working properly. The area of memory being tested is displayed on the monitor. The last (highest) number displayed on the monitor is the amount of memory installed in that computer.

In this case, the computer has 8192K (8MB) of memory installed.

MEMORY

640K   1024K   4G

| Conventional Memory (0-640K) | Memory Reserved for Computer (640K–1024K) | Extended Memory (1024K–4G) | |

Conventional Memory

Older microprocessors such as the 8088 could only use 1024K (1MB) of memory. 640K of that was reserved for the operating system, application programs and data. This area is known as "conventional memory".

The memory between 640K and 1024K is reserved for the computer's use.

Extended Memory

As programs become more complex, they require more memory. The newer microprocessors (examples: 80286, 80386 and 80486) use memory *extended* beyond conventional memory.

Note: Some MS-DOS programs use "expanded" memory instead of "extended" memory. For example, the Lotus 1-2-3 R2.x family of spreadsheet software uses expanded memory. Expanded memory is slower than extended memory.

Extended Memory Limits

80286 and 80386SX microprocessors can access up to 16MB of memory. 80386DX and 80486SX/DX/DX2 microprocessors can use up to 4GB of memory.

Memory Requirements

Different operating systems require different amounts of memory to run properly.

OPERATING SYSTEM		MEMORY REQUIRED IN MEGABYTES	
Manufacturer	Product Name	Normal Use	Heavy Use
Microsoft	MS-DOS	2	4
IBM	IBM-DOS	2	4
Microsoft	Windows	4	8
IBM	OS/2	6	10

GETTING STARTED	THE BASIC COMPUTER	INPUT/ OUTPUT	PROCESSING	STORAGE	PORTABLE COMPUTERS	OPERATING SYSTEMS	APPLICATION SOFTWARE	NETWORKING	GLOSSARY

MEMORY
CENTRAL PROCESSING UNIT

Adding Memory

Memory Cards

You can add memory to a computer by inserting memory cards called "SIMMs" (Single Inline Memory Module) into memory expansion slots.

Memory cards are designed to hold memory chips. Cards come in sizes of 256K, 1MB, 4MB, 8MB or 16MB.

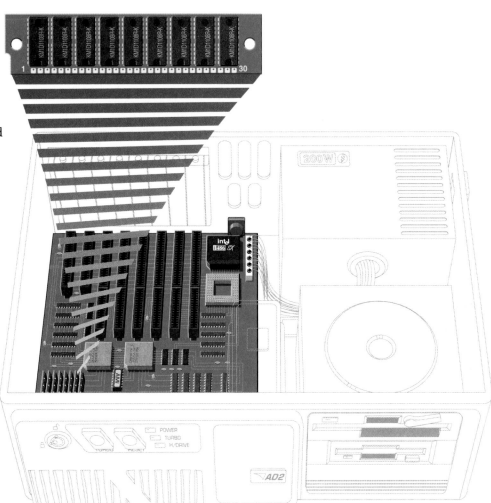

TIPS

◆ Memory expansion slots with metal brackets last longer than those made out of plastic.

◆ If you are purchasing a computer, check to make sure the motherboard can be upgraded to at least 16MB or 32MB for heavy-duty applications.

Memory cards should only be removed or inserted by computer technicians.

CENTRAL PROCESSING UNIT

The **CPU** (**Central Processing Unit**) is the "brain" behind the computer.

The CPU (also known as a microprocessor) is the single most important chip in the computer.

It has a direct effect on how fast programs run, how much memory can be accessed and ultimately how complex a job can be.

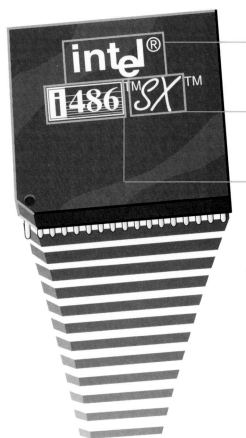

◆ **Manufacturer**

The name of the manufacturer which produced the chip. Intel chips are the most popular.

◆ **Type**

Microprocessors are available in several different types ranging from the "entry-level" SX to the high-performance DX2 .

◆ **Generation**

The major release of a microprocessor. Most computers manufactured today come with either an 80386 or 80486 microprocessor.

Note: The 80386 is also known as a "386". The 80486 is also known as "486".

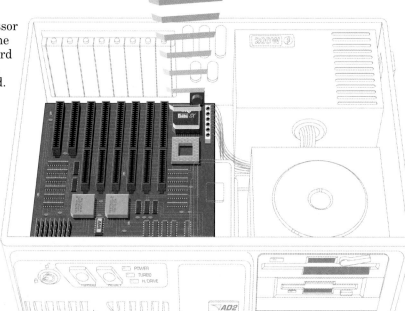

The microprocessor is installed on the main circuit board of the computer, the motherboard.

In 1993, Intel will introduce a new microprocessor called the Pentium™. It will contain 3.1 million transistors and outperform the 80486DX2 66-MHz microprocessor by 2 to 3 times.

Note: The 80486 microprocessor contains 1.2 million transistors.

GETTING STARTED	THE BASIC COMPUTER	INPUT/ OUTPUT	PROCESSING	STORAGE	PORTABLE COMPUTERS	OPERATING SYSTEMS	APPLICATION SOFTWARE	NETWORKING	GLOSSARY

MEMORY
CENTRAL PROCESSING UNIT

CPU Performance

CPU performance depends on three factors: speed, generation and type.

SPEED

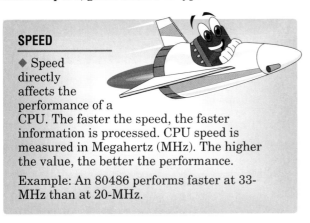

◆ Speed directly affects the performance of a CPU. The faster the speed, the faster information is processed. CPU speed is measured in Megahertz (MHz). The higher the value, the better the performance.

Example: An 80486 performs faster at 33-MHz than at 20-MHz.

TYPE

◆ Each generation of a CPU has a number of versions (types) available for various applications.

Type	Application
SX	Home
DX	Business
DX2	Power User
SL	Portable

GENERATION

◆ Each major generation of a CPU runs faster and offers new features and functions.

Example: A 20-MHz 80486 performs faster than a 33-MHz 80386.

Selecting a Microprocessor

As you move from left to right across this chart, CPU performance and cost both increase. Your final decision should be based on your budget and intended application.

Note: Before Intel officially named its next generation microprocessor Pentium, it was referred to as P5 or 80586.

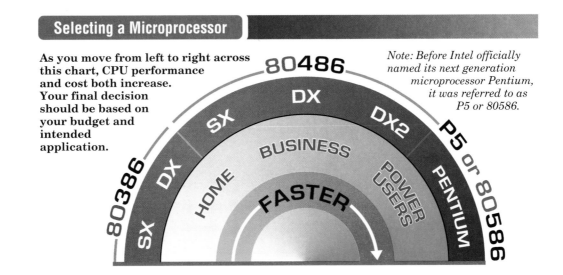

CENTRAL PROCESSING UNIT

OverDrive Upgrades

You can extend the lifespan of 80486SX and 80486DX computers by upgrading their microprocessors.

Intel's OverDrive microprocessors increase the performance of a computer up to 70%. There is nothing to buy except the OverDrive chip.

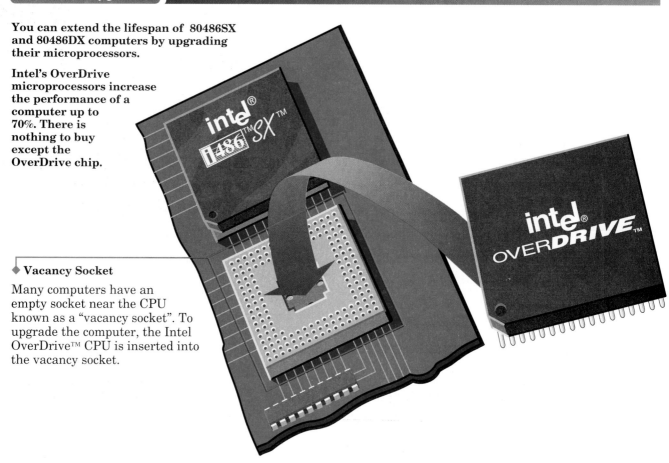

◆ Vacancy Socket

Many computers have an empty socket near the CPU known as a "vacancy socket". To upgrade the computer, the Intel OverDrive™ CPU is inserted into the vacancy socket.

Upgrading the microprocessor is a complex job and should only be performed by a computer technician.

80486 OVERDRIVE UPGRADE CHART

Original Microprocessor		Overdrive Speed (MHz)			
Type	Speed (MHz)	32	40	50	66
DX	33				●
DX	25			●	
SX	33				●
SX	25			●	
SX	20		●		
SX	16	●			

◆ *To the rest of your computer, an OverDrive microprocessor operates at the system speed. However, within the OverDrive microprocessor chip, it operates at **double** the system speed, for an overall performance improvement of up to 70%.*

GETTING STARTED	THE BASIC COMPUTER	INPUT/ OUTPUT	PROCESSING	STORAGE	PORTABLE COMPUTERS	OPERATING SYSTEMS	APPLICATION SOFTWARE	NETWORKING	GLOSSARY

MEMORY
CENTRAL PROCESSING UNIT

Certified Intel

Before purchasing a computer, ask if the system has been certified by Intel to work with an OverDrive CPU. Computers which have not been certified may not operate properly with an OverDrive chip.

ZIF Socket

ZIF (Zero Insertion Force) sockets make replacing the CPU easier on systems with no vacancy socket. When a small handle on the side of the socket is lifted, the CPU is pushed out. With this socket, the CPU can be removed without damaging it.

Math Coprocessors

A math coprocessor is a chip that works with the CPU to speed up complex calculations in graphics and scientific programs.

Software programs using a math coprocessor can run up to 500% faster.

Note: Check your program's user manual to see if a math coprocessor is required or supported.

$$3.14 \times \left(3a^2 \times 700\right) \div 1{,}298 - .654$$

$$+ 56.8977 \times \sqrt{32} \times \frac{6.78}{230}$$

$$756 \quad \div 98 \quad 08 \sqrt{45.76}$$

The newer coprocessors are more efficient.

Example: Even at the same speed, an 80486DX with a built-in math coprocessor processes data almost twice as fast as an older 80386DX with an external math coprocessor.

CENTRAL PROCESSING UNIT

Cache Memory

Cache memory can increase the speed of a computer up to 15%.

RAM MEMORY

Inside the computer, memory chips (called RAM or DRAM) temporarily hold programs and data for the CPU.

Since RAM chips are not fast enough to keep up with the CPU, it has to slow down and wait for instructions.

TIP Cache memory has the greatest impact on OverDrive and 80486DX2 microprocessors. It is recommended that 256K of cache memory be installed with these microprocessors.

CPU WITH BUILT-IN CACHE MEMORY

80486 SX, DX, DX2 and OverDrive microprocessors have 8K of super fast cache memory built-in. Commonly used instructions are retained by the cache and used when necessary.

Every time an instruction can be found in the cache (termed a "cache-hit"), a time consuming trip to the computer's RAM memory is avoided.

EXTERNAL CACHE MEMORY

On some computers, speed can be further increased by using a second level cache. The second level cache uses special memory chips called "SRAM".

Generally, the more second level cache memory installed, the greater the percentage of cache-hits and the faster the computer operates.

Note: DRAM stands for Dynamic Random Access Memory. It is also referred to as RAM.

*Note: SRAM stands for Static Random Access Memory. SRAM is **four times** faster than RAM.*

External cache memory is not required if you are only using MS-DOS applications.

MEMORY
CENTRAL PROCESSING UNIT

CPU Feature List

MICROPROCESSOR		FEATURES			SUITABLE FOR...		
Generation	Type	UPGRADABLE (OverDrive)	BUILT-IN 8K CACHE	BUILT-IN MATH CHIP	DOS	WINDOWS	OS/2
80486	DX2	✓	✓	✓	✓	✓	✓
80486	DX	✓	✓	✓	✓	✓	✓
80486	SX	✓	✓		✓	✓	✓
80386	DX				✓	✓	✓
80386	SX				✓	▽	▽

▽ *Although capable of using the indicated operating systems, performance will be poor and certain functions may not be supported.*

CPU Selection Chart

To Use For...	Generation	Type	Speed (MHz)
Home	80486	SX	25
Business	80486	DX	33
Power User	80486	DX2	66

BEFORE PURCHASING A COMPUTER...
TIPS

◆ Ask if the CPU can be upgraded and at what cost.

◆ Find out how much SRAM is installed, if more can be added and at what cost.

HOW FILES
ARE STORED

HOW FILES ARE SPECIFIED

In an office environment, people create, edit, review and organize paper documents (example: letters, worksheets, reports, etc.). These documents are stored in folders, which in turn are placed in cabinets. To retrieve a specific document, you must identify it by location (cabinet and folder) and then by name.

Computers work the same way. After creating a document, you must name and save it. During this process, you must tell the computer the drive (cabinet) and directory (folder) where you want to save the file.

Storage devices (example: hard drive, floppy drive) use a multi-level filing system to store and retrieve your files. The first level is called the root directory. From this directory, other subdirectories may be created. A typical multi-level filing system is illustrated on the next page.

File Specification

A file is specified by describing its drive, path, filename and extension.

c:	\winword\letters\	sales	.doc
DRIVE	**PATH**	**FILENAME**	**EXTENSION**
Tells the computer which drive the file is in.	Tells the computer the path through the directory structure to get to the file location.	The filename can contain up to 8 characters.	The extension can contain up to 3 characters. In some cases, it is omitted.

Note: OS/2 filenames can contain up to 254 characters if using the "High Performance File System" option.

The following characters are allowed:
◆ The letters A to Z, upper or lower case
◆ The digits 0 through 9
◆ The symbols ! @ # $ % ^ & - ( ) _ { } ~
◆ The filename cannot contain a . (period) or blank space

GETTING STARTED	THE BASIC COMPUTER	INPUT/ OUTPUT	PROCESSING	STORAGE	PORTABLE COMPUTERS	OPERATING SYSTEMS	APPLICATION SOFTWARE	NETWORKING	GLOSSARY

HOW FILES ARE STORED
HARD DISK DRIVE
FLOPPY DISK DRIVE
CD-ROM DRIVE
TAPE BACKUP UNIT

Using Directories to Organize Your Files

◆ Directories can contain files and/or paths to other directories. In this example, the root directory has paths to three subdirectories called \dos, \winword and \windows.

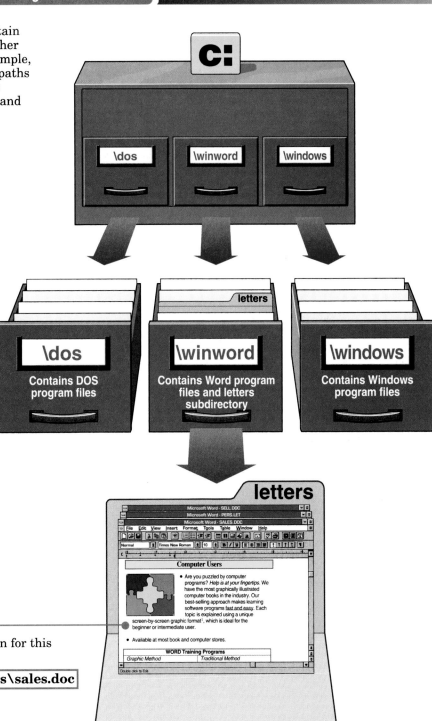

◆ The file specification for this data file is:

c:\winword\letters\sales.doc

HARD DISK DRIVE

What is a Hard Disk Drive?

Unlike electronic memory (RAM) which forgets everything when the power is turned off, hard disk drives (also called hard drives) store programs and data permanently. Most computers are equipped with at least one hard drive.

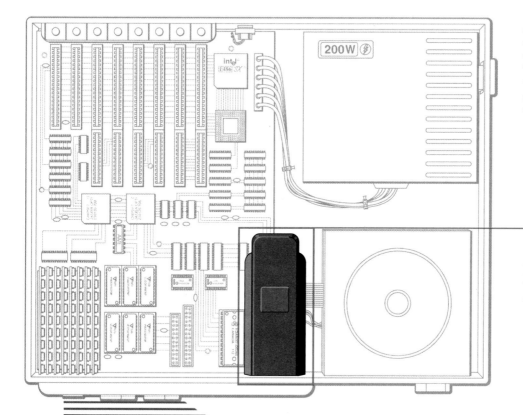

Note: Ever record a home movie with a camcorder? The movie is stored permanently on a magnetic tape cassette.

The computer stores information much the same way on a hard disk.

◆ Most hard drives are installed inside the computer case. External hard drives that connect to the computer by a cable are also available.

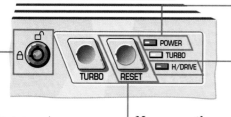

◆ Never move the computer when the power light is **on**.

◆ Be careful not to bump the computer when the hard drive activity light is **on**.

◆ To prevent access to files stored on your hard disk drive, lock the computer when you are away from your desk.

◆ Never use the reset button unless all the information on your screen has first been saved to the hard disk drive.

DID YOU KNOW?

Data is magnetically stored inside the hard drive on rotating disks. As most hard drives have disks which cannot be removed from the drive, they are also called "fixed disk drives".

Recently, hard drives with removable disks have been introduced. They are called "removable hard disk drives".

HOW FILES ARE STORED
HARD DISK DRIVE
FLOPPY DISK DRIVE
CD-ROM DRIVE
TAPE BACKUP UNIT

How a Hard Disk Drive Works

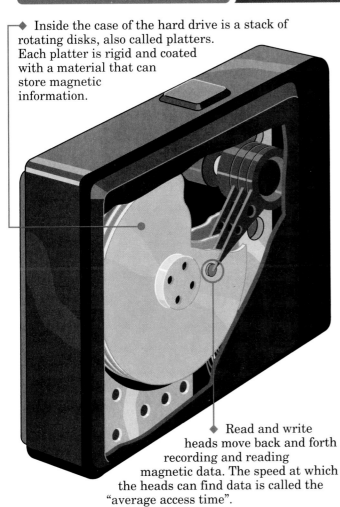

◆ Inside the case of the hard drive is a stack of rotating disks, also called platters. Each platter is rigid and coated with a material that can store magnetic information.

◆ Read and write heads move back and forth recording and reading magnetic data. The speed at which the heads can find data is called the "average access time".

TWO TYPES OF HARD DRIVES

Hard drives "talk" to the computer using one of two common languages.

IDE

"Inexpensive and good for most home and business applications" sums up IDE hard drives.

◆ Each IDE controller can operate one or two hard drives. Installation is fast and does not require any special software.

◆ Most motherboards have a built-in IDE connector, so it is not necessary to purchase an expansion card.

SCSI

"Powerful, expensive and made for power users" describes the second common way of connecting a hard drive.

◆ SCSI (pronounced scuzzy) controllers can operate up to 7 hard drives at the same time. SCSI controllers can also operate other peripherals such as tape backup units and CD-ROM drives. Installation is complex and requires special "software drivers".

◆ As most computers do not have built-in SCSI connectors, a SCSI expansion card will have to be installed.

Note: SCSI stands for Small Computer System Interface.

Since the read and write heads float above the platters on nothing more than a thin cushion of air, you will want to make sure that your computer is not bumped, jarred or moved while the hard disk is in operation.

HARD DISK DRIVE

Disk Cache

Disk caching can increase the hard drive's performance by up to 20 times. Every time the computer requests data from the hard drive, it copies that data to the disk cache. The next time the computer needs that same data, it retrieves it from the disk cache, instead of the slow hard drive.

Note: Most operating systems include a cache program (example: Windows 3.1 uses a cache program called "SMARTDrive 4.0").

HARD DRIVE

Hard drives operate very slowly compared to the computer's CPU and electronic memory (RAM).

Every time any data is retrieved from the hard drive, the CPU is forced to wait, slowing down its overall performance.

◆ For maximum performance, have a computer expert optimize the disk cache size.

TIP

CPU

DISK CACHE MEMORY

Disk cache programs set aside an area in the computer's electronic memory (RAM). Each time any data is read from the hard drive, a copy is stored in the cache. When the cache is full, the most recently-entered data "bumps out" the oldest data in the cache.

When the CPU requests data from the hard drive, the cache program checks the disk cache. If the data is found there, it is sent to the CPU. Each time the CPU finds data in the disk cache, it eliminates a time-consuming trip to the hard drive.

HOW FILES ARE STORED
HARD DISK DRIVE
FLOPPY DISK DRIVE
CD-ROM DRIVE
TAPE BACKUP UNIT

How to Choose a Hard Drive

CAPACITY

The amount of programs and data a hard drive can store is measured in Megabytes (MB). The capacity of the drive is the single most important consideration in its selection.

Always purchase a hard drive at least 50% larger than what you think you will need. In this case, the bigger the better.

CAPACITY IN DOWN TO EARTH TERMS

If a typed page contains 1,000 characters (or 1K), then a 200MB hard drive contains the equivalent of 200,000 pages.

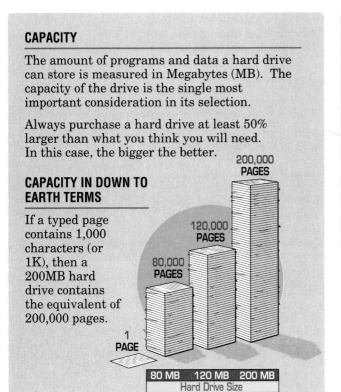

200,000 PAGES

120,000 PAGES

80,000 PAGES

1 PAGE

80 MB	120 MB	200 MB
Hard Drive Size		

SPEED

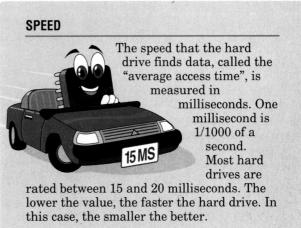

The speed that the hard drive finds data, called the "average access time", is measured in milliseconds. One millisecond is 1/1000 of a second. Most hard drives are rated between 15 and 20 milliseconds. The lower the value, the faster the hard drive. In this case, the smaller the better.

15 MS

RECOMMENDATIONS	
Application	Minimum Recommended Capacity
Home	80MB
Business	120MB
Power User	200MB Plus

TIP

◆ Always purchase the largest capacity hard drive and be less concerned about the drive's "average access time".

FLOPPY DISK DRIVE

What is a Floppy Disk Drive?

Floppy disk drives store programs and data onto removable media known as diskettes (or floppy disks). Floppy disk drives operate slower and have significantly less capacity than hard disk drives.

FLOPPY DISK DRIVES ARE AVAILABLE IN TWO SIZES

The larger size works with 5.25" diskettes.

The smaller size works with 3.5" diskettes.

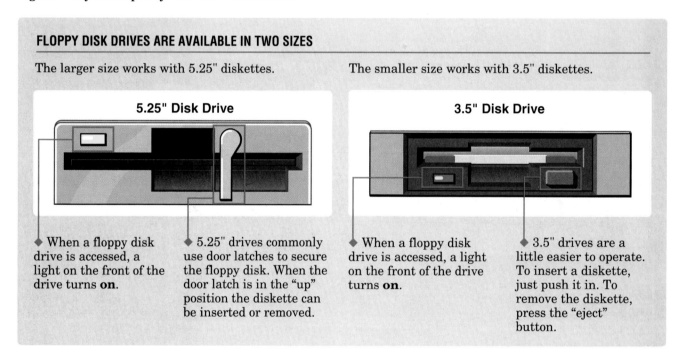

5.25" Disk Drive

3.5" Disk Drive

◆ When a floppy disk drive is accessed, a light on the front of the drive turns **on**.

◆ 5.25" drives commonly use door latches to secure the floppy disk. When the door latch is in the "up" position the diskette can be inserted or removed.

◆ When a floppy disk drive is accessed, a light on the front of the drive turns **on**.

◆ 3.5" drives are a little easier to operate. To insert a diskette, just push it in. To remove the diskette, press the "eject" button.

Types of Diskettes

Disk drives store data on removable diskettes.

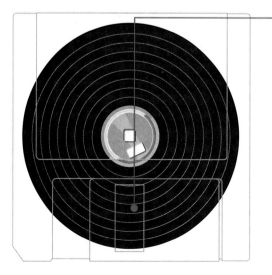

◆ Inside the protective covering of a diskette is a flexible (floppy) platter (disk). Diskettes known as "high-density" can store more information than "double-density" diskettes of the same size.

Note: Diskettes are also called floppy disks.

| GETTING STARTED | THE BASIC COMPUTER | INPUT/ OUTPUT | PROCESSING | STORAGE | PORTABLE COMPUTERS | OPERATING SYSTEMS | APPLICATION SOFTWARE | NETWORKING | GLOSSARY |

HOW FILES ARE STORED
HARD DISK DRIVE
FLOPPY DISK DRIVE
CD-ROM DRIVE
TAPE BACKUP UNIT

FORMATTING

Diskettes must be prepared for use (or formatted) before you can store any data on them.

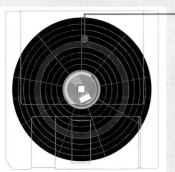

◆ Formatting divides a diskette into concentric tracks and wedge-shaped sectors.

It is done for the same reason that library shelves are organized by category and number, so books can be found easily.

The drive locates data by using the tracks and sectors on the diskette.

CAPACITY

Different amounts of data can be stored on diskettes of different types and sizes.

Type	Capacity	
	5.25"	3.5"
Double-Density (DD)	360K	720K
High-Density (HD)	1.2MB	1.44MB

Chess Disk V. 2.0

5.25" DISK DRIVE

Double-density 5.25" drives divide a diskette into 40 tracks. High-density drives use narrower read/write heads to divide a diskette into 80 tracks.

High-density drives can read double-density diskettes, but should not be used to format or write to them.

Type of Drive	Can Use	
	Double-Density	High-Density
Double-Density	●	
High-Density	●	●

● *Read Only*

MicroFLOPPY Double Sided

3.5" DISK DRIVE

Although high-density 3.5" drives divide a diskette into the same number of tracks as double-density drives, they "cram" twice as much information into each track.

High-density drives can both read and write to double-density diskettes.

Type of Drive	Can Use	
	Double-Density	High-Density
Double-Density	●	
High-Density	●	●

FLOPPY DISK DRIVE

A Closer Look at Diskettes

Programs and data are stored by the disk drive on a diskette (or floppy disk). Diskettes are commonly used to transfer information from one computer to another or to make a backup copy of a hard drive's contents.

5.25" DISKETTE

Chess Disk V. 2.0

◆ Most diskettes have a label that describes their contents. Use a soft-tipped felt marker to write on the label, since a pen or pencil may damage the media under the protective cover.

◆ Diskettes can be "write-protected" to prevent any information from being erased or recorded on the diskette. To write-protect a 5.25" diskette, you place a small sticker over a notch on the diskette.

Not Write-Protected   **Write-Protected**

3.5" DISKETTE

MicroFLOPPY
Double Sided

◆ 3.5" diskettes have built-in write-protect tabs. Programs and data can only be recorded and erased from the disk when the tab is in the "Not Write-Protected" position.

Not Write-Protected   **Write-Protected**

◆ Improved features of 3.5" diskettes include sturdier plastic, shirt-pocket size, and a metal covering to protect the media from finger marks, scratches and dust.

HOW FILES ARE STORED
HARD DISK DRIVE
FLOPPY DISK DRIVE
CD-ROM DRIVE
TAPE BACKUP UNIT

Inserting a Diskette into a Disk Drive

Note: To insert a 5.25" diskette, follow the same steps and then move the door latch down.

1 Insert the diskette into the drive, label side up and metal shutter first.

2 Push the diskette gently into the disk drive. Most drives will make a "click" sound when the diskette is fully inserted.

Never insert or remove a diskette when the disk activity light is **on**.

Purchasing a Box of Diskettes

Before visiting your local computer store, write down the specifications for the diskettes you require. It is a good idea to keep some formatted (ready-to-use) diskettes near your computer.

◆ Physical size of the diskettes. Make sure that they are the same size as the type of disk drive you have.

◆ Prepared for use (formatted). All diskettes need to be formatted before they can be used.

◆ Early models of computers stored information on one side of a diskette. These diskettes were known as "Single-Sided (SS)". Modern disk drives store information on both sides of the diskette and are known as "Double-Sided (DS)".

◆ "High-Density" diskettes are labeled "HD" while "Double-Density" diskettes are labeled "DD".

What is a CD-ROM?

CD-ROM drives read programs and data stored on removable CD-ROM discs. These discs can hold large amounts of information (example: encyclopedias) which cannot be altered.

Note: Only CD-ROM drives which incorporate special software can play audio compact discs (CDs).

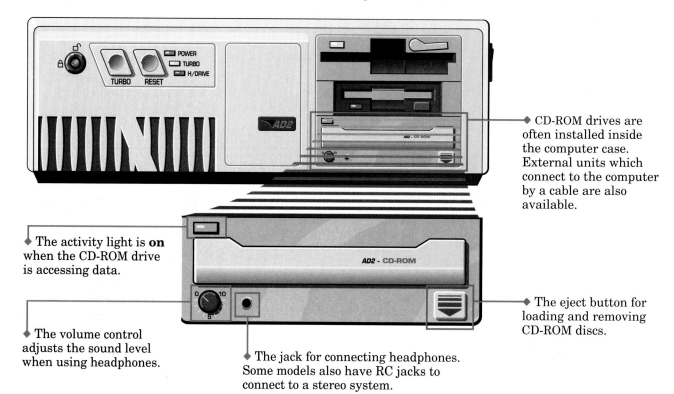

◆ CD-ROM drives are often installed inside the computer case. External units which connect to the computer by a cable are also available.

◆ The activity light is **on** when the CD-ROM drive is accessing data.

◆ The volume control adjusts the sound level when using headphones.

◆ The eject button for loading and removing CD-ROM discs.

◆ The jack for connecting headphones. Some models also have RC jacks to connect to a stereo system.

CD-ROM Discs

CD-ROMs are hard, plastic, silver–colored platters, 5.25" in diameter. Although the discs are designed to last indefinitely, finger marks or scratches can damage the disc's surface.

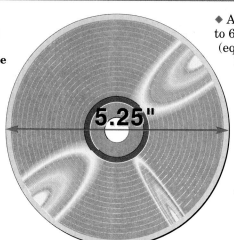

5.25"

◆ A single CD-ROM can hold up to 650MB of information (equivalent to 1,000 300-page books).

◆ Just like musical CDs, CD-ROMs can only play pre-recorded information.

◆ **CD-ROM** stands for **C**ompact **D**isc-**R**ead **O**nly **M**emory, which means you cannot save your own files on a CD-ROM.

HOW FILES ARE STORED
HARD DISK DRIVE
FLOPPY DISK DRIVE
CD-ROM DRIVE
TAPE BACKUP UNIT

CD-ROM Applications

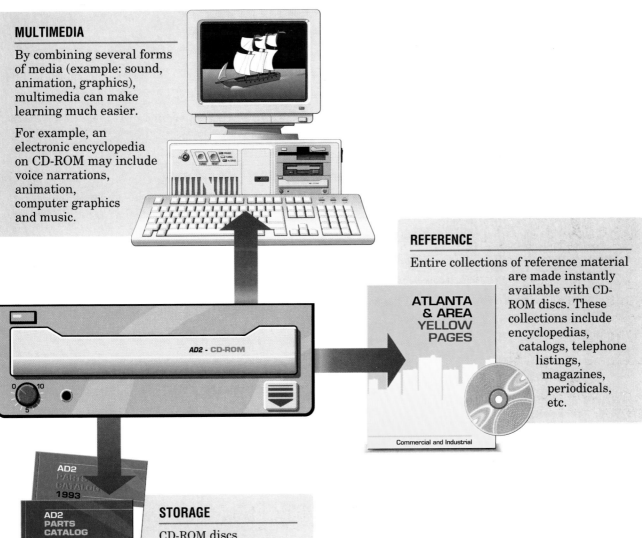

MULTIMEDIA

By combining several forms of media (example: sound, animation, graphics), multimedia can make learning much easier.

For example, an electronic encyclopedia on CD-ROM may include voice narrations, animation, computer graphics and music.

REFERENCE

Entire collections of reference material are made instantly available with CD-ROM discs. These collections include encyclopedias, catalogs, telephone listings, magazines, periodicals, etc.

ATLANTA & AREA YELLOW PAGES

Commercial and Industrial

STORAGE

CD-ROM discs containing company records, discontinued products, etc., can be accessed quickly and at low cost.

AD2 PARTS CATALOG 1993
AD2 PARTS CATALOG 1994

AD2 - CD-ROM

◆ The average access time of a CD-ROM drive used for multimedia should be 350 milliseconds or less. Animation sequences in multimedia applications appear "choppy" on slower drives.

TIP

TAPE BACKUP UNIT

What is a Tape Backup Unit?

Hard drive "disasters" range from a single file being "corrupted" to a complete failure of the drive. To protect against losing any of your files, you should make a backup copy of all your data.

◆ Small files or groups of files less than 1MB can be backed up to a floppy disk. For larger files or groups of files, it is more convenient to use a tape backup unit.

◆ Tape backup units provide a quick, convenient method of backing up a hard drive. Units which use "DC-2000 minicartridges" can store the contents of most hard drives and are relatively inexpensive.

Where a Tape Backup Unit is Installed

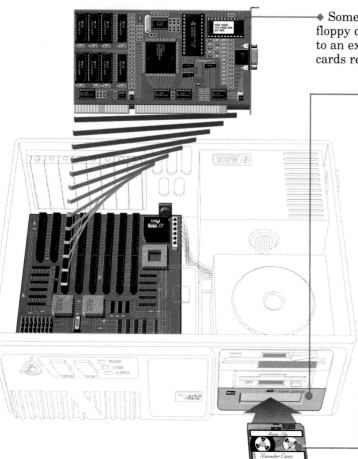

◆ Some tape backup units connect to an existing floppy disk drive controller, while others connect to an expansion card. "Accelerated" expansion cards reduce backup time by 50%.

◆ Tape backup units are available as either internal or external models. Internal units should be installed by a computer technician.

◆ To make a backup, you insert a tape cartridge into the tape drive. Tapes must be formatted (prepared) before you can use them. To save time, you can buy tape cartridges already pre-formatted.

◆ Use a tape cartridge which is big enough to store more information than you are backing up.

Trust us! There is nothing worse than waiting around to swap cartridges.

TIP

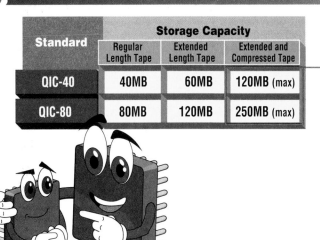

HOW FILES ARE STORED
HARD DISK DRIVE
FLOPPY DISK DRIVE
CD-ROM DRIVE
TAPE BACKUP UNIT

Storage Capacities

Always use tape backup units certified as "QIC-40" or "QIC-80" to ensure compatibility with other tape drives.

Note: QIC stands for Quarter-Inch Cartridge.

Standard	Storage Capacity		
	Regular Length Tape	Extended Length Tape	Extended and Compressed Tape
QIC-40	40MB	60MB	120MB (max)
QIC-80	80MB	120MB	250MB (max)

◆ "Compression" is an optional feature on many tape backup units. This reduces the size of your files to be backed up by "compressing" their information. Compression ratios vary for different types of data, so the values in the table are only averages.

Backup Strategies

Always backup frequently. Ask yourself: how much work can I afford to lose? If you can only afford to lose a day's worth of work, then make a daily backup.

If your files do not change very often during the week and you can afford to lose a week's worth of work, then backup weekly.

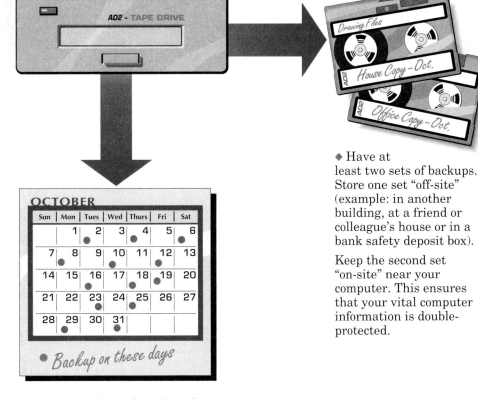

◆ Have at least two sets of backups. Store one set "off-site" (example: in another building, at a friend or colleague's house or in a bank safety deposit box).

Keep the second set "on-site" near your computer. This ensures that your vital computer information is double-protected.

◆ Make a backup schedule and stick to it! Hard drive disasters always seem to happen right after you miss a scheduled backup.

What is a Portable Computer?

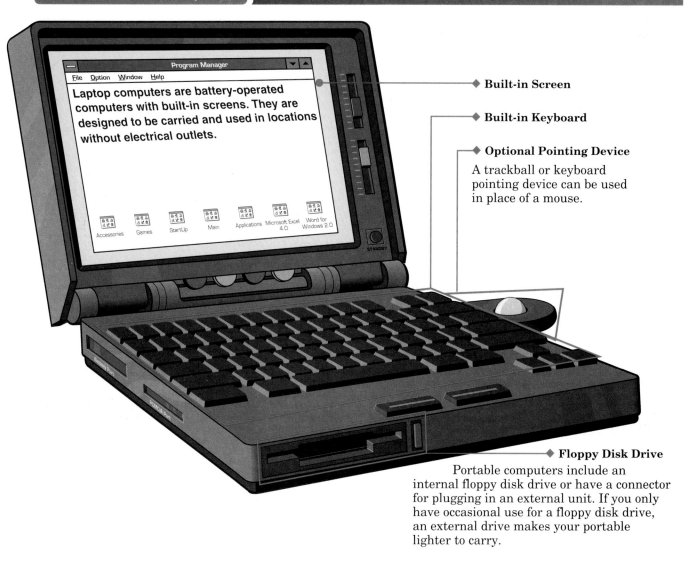

Program Manager

File   Option   Window   Help

Laptop computers are battery-operated computers with built-in screens. They are designed to be carried and used in locations without electrical outlets.

Accessories   Games   StartUp   Main   Applications   Microsoft Excel 4.0   Word for Windows 2.0

STANDBY

◆ **Built-in Screen**

◆ **Built-in Keyboard**

◆ **Optional Pointing Device**
A trackball or keyboard pointing device can be used in place of a mouse.

◆ **Floppy Disk Drive**
Portable computers include an internal floppy disk drive or have a connector for plugging in an external unit. If you only have occasional use for a floppy disk drive, an external drive makes your portable lighter to carry.

TIPS

◆ Look for a keyboard which has cursor control keys arranged in the shape of an inverted "T", with separate "PgUp" and "PgDn" keys.

◆ The floppy disk drive should be located at the front of the portable for easy access.

Portable computers are grouped by weight. As a rule of thumb, price goes up as the size gets smaller (except for palmtops, which may offer limited functions).

Classification	Weight
LAPTOP	8–10 lb
NOTEBOOK	6–8 lb
SUB-NOTEBOOK	2–6 lb
PALMTOP	Under 2 lb

Screens

Portable computers have built-in, energy-efficient screens designed to be used "on-the-road".

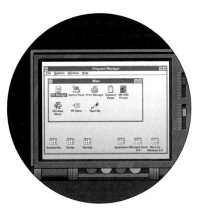

VGA STANDARD

Portable computers should offer at least the VGA standard (640 by 480 pixels) and be capable of displaying at least 16 colors or shades of grey.

BACKLIGHTING

Most screens include a built-in "light" behind the screen. The light makes for easier viewing in low-light conditions but shortens the battery life.

TILT/SWIVEL

LCD (**L**iquid **C**rystal **D**isplays) are only legible if viewed from the correct angle. Most screens can be tilted as required, and some can also be swiveled.

Types of Screens

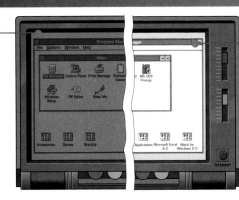

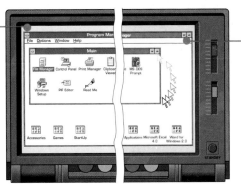

◆ Gas Plasma

Gas plasma screens display graphics fast enough to avoid "ghosting". As gas plasma screens consume more power than LCD screens and are harder to view in sunlight, they are not very popular.

◆ Passive Matrix LCD

Passive matrix screens are low cost, energy-efficient and available in monochrome or color. They display graphics very slowly, which results in "ghosting". They also lack the color depth of active matrix screens.

◆ Active Matrix LCD

Active matrix screens display graphics faster, have more color depth and are available in monochrome and color. Compared to passive matrix displays, they cost more, weigh more and use more power.

◆ "Ghosting"

"Ghosting" refers to the shadows of graphics which linger on the screen. The "ghosting effect" is most noticeable with moving images. It is not uncommon to see "ghost pointers" trailing a mouse pointer as it moves around a passive matrix screen.

EXPANSION

Some portable computers come with one or more expansion slots. Expansion slots accommodate expansion cards which extend the capabilities of the portable computer.

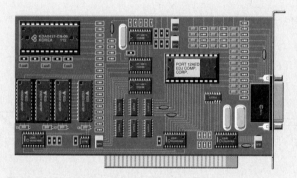

Regular computer expansion cards are too bulky and use too much power to fit inside a portable computer.

Instead, special credit card sized expansion cards are used. The "standard" for expansion slots and cards is called "**P**ersonal **C**omputer **M**emory **C**ard **I**nternational **A**ssociation" or "**PCMCIA**". A PCMCIA slot can accept a variety of PCMCIA cards from various manufacturers.

Note: Portables whose expansion slots do not conform to the PCMCIA standard can only use that manufacturer's expansion cards.

Types of PCMCIA Expansion Cards

Type I cards (3.3mm thick)

USED FOR

◆ Memory Cards
◆ Software Application Cards

Can be used in Type I, II or III expansion slots.

Type II cards (5mm thick)

USED FOR

◆ Modem and Fax Cards
◆ LAN Cards
◆ Type I Uses

Can be used in Type II or III expansion slots.

Type III cards (10.5mm thick)

USED FOR

◆ Miniature Hard Drives
◆ Type I and Type II Uses

Can only be used in Type III expansion slots.

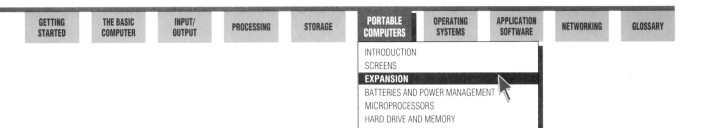

INTRODUCTION
SCREENS
EXPANSION
BATTERIES AND POWER MANAGEMENT
MICROPROCESSORS
HARD DRIVE AND MEMORY

Connections

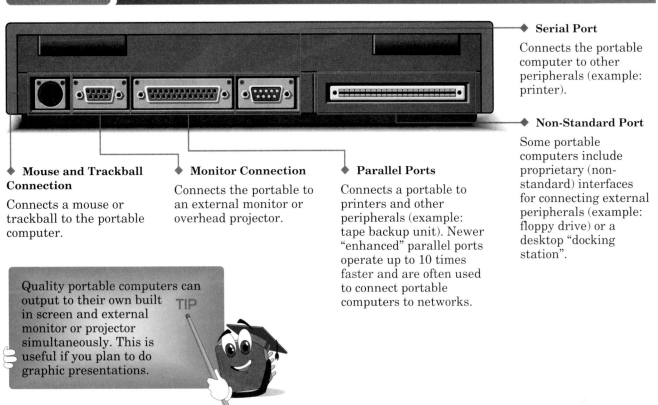

♦ **Serial Port**

Connects the portable computer to other peripherals (example: printer).

♦ **Non-Standard Port**

Some portable computers include proprietary (non-standard) interfaces for connecting external peripherals (example: floppy drive) or a desktop "docking station".

♦ **Mouse and Trackball Connection**

Connects a mouse or trackball to the portable computer.

♦ **Monitor Connection**

Connects the portable to an external monitor or overhead projector.

♦ **Parallel Ports**

Connects a portable to printers and other peripherals (example: tape backup unit). Newer "enhanced" parallel ports operate up to 10 times faster and are often used to connect portable computers to networks.

Quality portable computers can output to their own built in screen and external monitor or projector simultaneously. This is useful if you plan to do graphic presentations.

TIP

Docking Station

If you require a full-sized computer in addition to a portable, consider purchasing a docking station.

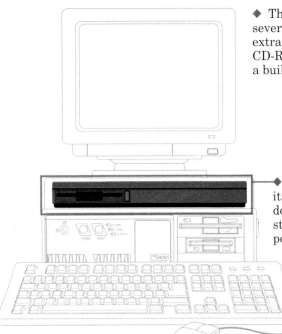

♦ The docking station provides several expansion slots, room for extra storage devices (example: CD-ROM), a full-sized monitor and a built-in power supply.

♦ The portable computer, with its lid shut, is inserted into the docking station. The docking station continually charges the portable's battery as it is used.

Docking stations and portables only work together if they are from the same manufacturer.

TIP

BATTERIES AND POWER MANAGEMENT

Batteries

Portable computers are designed to operate from internal batteries.

QUICK CHANGE BATTERIES

Most portable computers can have fresh or recharged batteries inserted while the computer is running. Some portables may require you to save your work and shut down the computer before you can insert fresh batteries.

CHARGE WHILE USING

Not all portable computers can recharge their battery packs while you use the computer. For most flexibility, it is best to purchase a portable that can do so.

AC (POWER OUTLET) TRANSFORMER

Look for a small, lightweight transformer. If you will be using the portable computer in different countries, you may wish to enquire about voltage converters.

TIPS
- ◆ Keep a charged battery pack handy– just in case!
- ◆ With the proper adapter, the battery pack can be recharged from a car's cigarette lighter.

Types of Batteries

Type of Battery	Rechargeable	"Memory Effect"
Nickel Cadmium	YES	YES
Metal Hydride	YES	NO

◆ Repeatedly recharging a partially-depleted Nickel Cadmium battery can reduce its capacity to hold power. As a result of this "memory effect", portable computers will not run as long with older battery packs as with new packs.

Power Management

◆ POWER CHARGE INDICATOR

Quality portables have displays which indicate the amount of battery life remaining. Low-cost units may provide only "warning" beeps from the internal speaker as power runs low.

◆ STAND-BY MODE

Pressing the "stand-by" button puts the computer to "sleep" after saving all your work. Pressing the button a second time "wakes-up" the portable computer and restores the display to how it was when you first pressed the button.

◆ ADVANCED POWER MANAGEMENT (APM)

Portable computers use many "tricks" to conserve power. Since the display and hard drive consume up to 70% of the available power, they are shut down when not required. APM also shuts down other parts of the portable (example: serial ports, CPU) when they are not being used.

◆ AUTO-SHUTDOWN

Quality portables have an auto-shutdown feature. Just before the battery runs out, the computer saves all your information and then shuts itself down. When the computer has been recharged or connected to a power source, it automatically restores the display to how it was before the auto-shutdown occurred.

SL Microprocessors

In addition to the "regular" microprocessors available for portable computers, special low power "SL" microprocessors designed to conserve power are available.

80386SL

In addition to the features of an 80386SX, 80386SL microprocessors include:

◆ Built-in power management features to conserve battery power. For instance, the 80386SL will reduce its speed and power consumption on tasks which do not require full processing power.

◆ By integrating many "support" chips into the microprocessor, the motherboard is smaller and more compact.

80486SL

In addition to the features of the 80386SL, 80486SL microprocessors also include:

◆ 80486DX capabilities including a built-in math coprocessor and 8K cache.

◆ Further reductions in power consumption of 25 to 50% (extending the battery life 1 to 4 hours).

◆ 80486SL motherboards can be up to 60% smaller than the already miniature 80386SL motherboards.

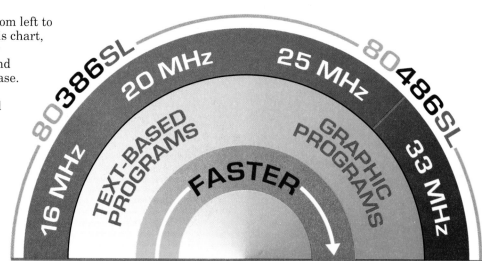

As you move from left to right across this chart, microprocessor performance and cost both increase. Your final decision should be based on your budget and intended application.

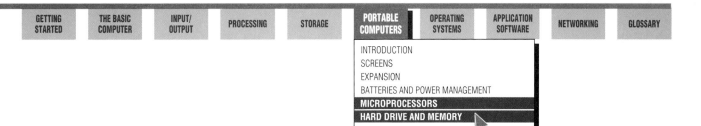

Hard Drive Concerns

Hard drives designed for portable computers are less bulky and power-hungry than the "ordinary" hard drives in full-sized computers.

◆ "Flash memory" cards are faster, more rugged and consume less power than a hard drive.

These cards can replace or supplement the existing hard drive. Flash memory cards fit into PCMCIA expansion slots.

◆ Some hard drives are removable, which is ideal if the portable is shared among several users. By storing different types of information on different drives or by assigning different drives to different people, hard drive space is virtually unlimited.

◆ If you are buying a portable with a hard drive which cannot be removed, choose a drive of 80MB or more. Avoid units with only 40 or 60MB, as they quickly fill up.

Always store removable hard drives with important information in a secure location when not in use.

HARD DRIVE AND MEMORY

Hard Disk Compression

By compressing information on a hard drive, you can store more information on it (example: a compressed 60MB hard drive stores almost as much data as a normal 120MB hard drive).

Using compression on a portable computer enables you to bring more programs and data "on the road" with you.

◆ As the information is stored to the hard drive, it is compressed to save space. Under ideal circumstances, a hard drive using compression can store twice as much as a hard drive with no compression.

Compression works by substituting shorter characters for longer strings of characters.

For example, if "#" = "THE":

THEre THEy went to THE
(uncompressed = 22 characters)

#re #y went to #
(compressed = 16 characters).

The compressed string is almost 30% shorter.

◆ When the information is used, it is automatically decompressed as required. As this process is performed by the computer, it does not require you to do anything.

Using Memory to Increase Battery Life

Add as much electronic memory to your portable as possible to minimize your hard drive use. The less you use the hard drive, the longer the batteries will last.

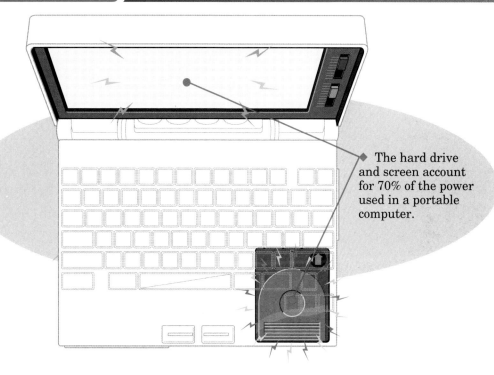

◆ The hard drive and screen account for 70% of the power used in a portable computer.

◆ You can also minimize your hard drive use by increasing the software cache size.

Example: A portable computer running Windows should ideally have a software cache size of 5MB with 3MB reserved for program use.

Note: For information on software caching refer to page 50.

◆ For maximum battery life, purchase a portable computer equipped with an "SL" rather than an "SX", "DX" or "DX2" microprocessor.

TIP

INTRODUCTION

What is an Operating System?

An operating system might be described as the computer's master control program, or the traffic cop that keeps everything flowing smoothly.

◆ Actually, the operating system is a collection of programs to manage files, deal with peripheral devices such as your printer and help you control the computer.

Software Version

Computer software usually has a two-digit version number. To get the most out of your computer, always use the latest software version.

Disk 1 - For DOS
Version
5.0

◆ The digit before the decimal point indicates a major software release. Each major release is a complete overhaul of the software.

◆ The digit after the decimal point indicates a minor software revision. Minor revisions often include "bug-fixes" (corrections to mistakes in the software) and a limited number of new features.

| GETTING STARTED | THE BASIC COMPUTER | INPUT/ OUTPUT | PROCESSING | STORAGE | PORTABLE COMPUTERS | OPERATING SYSTEMS | APPLICATION SOFTWARE | NETWORKING | GLOSSARY |

INTRODUCTION
MS-DOS
WINDOWS
OS/2

What the Operating System does

When you first turn on your computer, it checks to ensure that its internal devices, electronic memory and peripherals are functioning properly. Following this test the operating system is loaded.

◆ The operating system acts somewhat like a traffic cop. It enforces basic rules that all other programs must follow.

Programs, operating under the watchful eye of the operating system, perform tasks such as word processing, spreadsheet analysis, etc. When a program inputs or outputs data it does so under the control of the operating system.

The operating system controls how a program interacts with you.

For example, Windows and OS/2 applications use colorful graphics called "icons" to make things easier to learn and use.

The operating system also provides a basic set of programs called utilities.

These utilities are used to create directories, copy files, check for hard disk errors and format (prepare for use) diskettes.

71

MS-DOS

What is MS-DOS?

MS-DOS is the most popular personal computer operating system. You enter MS-DOS commands from either the "command prompt" or the easy-to-use "MS-DOS Shell".

Command Prompt

Since the command prompt was the only way to operate MS-DOS for many years, it is widely used. Although powerful, computer novices find it difficult to learn.

◆ The prompt indicates your current drive and directory (similar to a cabinet and folder). In this example, the hard drive "C:" and the directory "LETTERS" are active.

◆ These are filenames. A filename can contain up to 11 characters.

Note: When you type an MS-DOS command (example: dir) it operates on files in the current or active directory only.

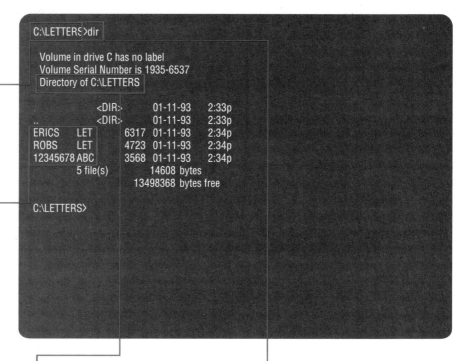

```
C:\LETTERS>dir

Volume in drive C has no label
Volume Serial Number is 1935-6537
Directory of C:\LETTERS

              <DIR>        01-11-93    2:33p
..            <DIR>        01-11-93    2:33p
ERICS    LET     6317     01-11-93    2:34p
ROBS     LET     4723     01-11-93    2:34p
12345678 ABC     3568     01-11-93    2:34p
         5 file(s)         14608 bytes
                        13498368 bytes free

C:\LETTERS>
```

◆ Directories are used to group files (example: programs, data).

◆ You enter commands to perform a function or start a program. The command "dir" (for directory) displays all the files in the current directory.

TIPS

◆ Most dealers install MS-DOS for new users at no extra charge.

◆ Make sure that you receive the original MS-DOS disks, registration form and all documentation for future reference.

INTRODUCTION
MS-DOS
WINDOWS
OS/2

MS-DOS Shell

The MS-DOS Shell provides an easy, graphical approach to using most commands.

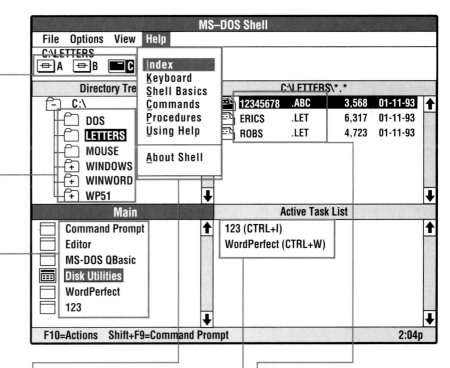

◆ Available drives (example: floppy disk drives, hard drives) are grouped together and displayed as icons. The drive currently in use is highlighted (drive "C:" in this example).

◆ Folders are used to group the files (example: applications, data) stored in the current drive.

◆ Programs are grouped together to make them easier to work with.

Note: A mouse makes it easier to use the MS-DOS Shell.

The terms "folder" and "directory" mean the same thing.

The terms "program" and "application" mean the same thing.

◆ Pull-down menus are used to group related commands.

◆ Names used to represent files can contain up to 11 characters.

◆ The "task swapper" switches between programs quickly. Only one program can operate at a time. The other programs are temporarily suspended until you switch to one of them.

◆ The MS-DOS Shell can be "programmed" to start automatically when the computer is turned on. This can be done either during your initial installation or at a later date.

WINDOWS

What is Microsoft Windows?

Microsoft Windows is an operating system that works with MS-DOS to make a computer easier to use. Windows adds powerful features not available with MS-DOS.

Note: To take advantage of all the Microsoft Windows features, you need a mouse.

◆ Windows can run more than one program at the same time. This is called multitasking.

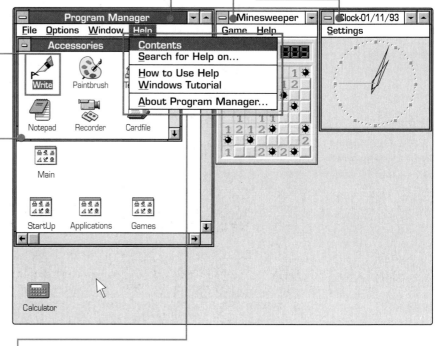

◆ Icons represent files (example: applications, data). The name of each file is listed below each icon.

◆ Windows are used to organize icons.

Note: Windows can be moved, sized, opened and closed as required. This allows each user to set up their own desktop as they prefer.

◆ Pull-down menus are used to organize related commands. Many commands also have "shortcuts" (example: you can ask for "help" by simply pressing F1).

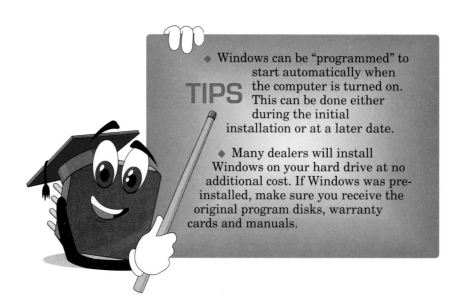

TIPS

◆ Windows can be "programmed" to start automatically when the computer is turned on. This can be done either during the initial installation or at a later date.

◆ Many dealers will install Windows on your hard drive at no additional cost. If Windows was pre-installed, make sure you receive the original program disks, warranty cards and manuals.

| GETTING STARTED | THE BASIC COMPUTER | INPUT/ OUTPUT | PROCESSING | STORAGE | PORTABLE COMPUTERS | OPERATING SYSTEMS | APPLICATION SOFTWARE | NETWORKING | GLOSSARY |

INTRODUCTION
MS-DOS
WINDOWS
OS/2

A large number of applications and utilities are included with Microsoft Windows, including the "Write", "Cardfile" and "Paintbrush" programs shown below.

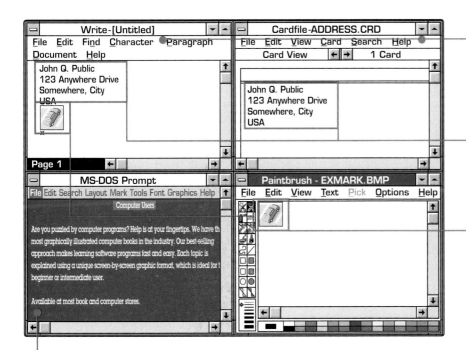

◆ The consistent "look and feel" among Windows applications makes them easier to learn and use. For instance, pull-down menus work the same way in every application.

◆ Cut and paste allows you to cut (or copy) text and graphics from one application and paste them into another.

◆ **O**bject **L**inking and **E**mbedding (**OLE**) enables one or more objects (example: a graphic) to be linked or embedded into other documents. As information changes in one object, it is automatically updated in the linked or embedded object.

When you double-click a linked or embedded object, the application which created the object is started. This allows you to edit objects from within a document without having to open the applications which originally created them.

◆ You can also run MS-DOS applications in addition to Windows applications.

◆ For best performance, make sure that your computer has at least 4MB of electronic memory (RAM). If performance is slow or you get memory related errors, add another 4MB of RAM.

OS/2

What is OS/2?

OS/2 is an operating system that can run MS-DOS and Windows applications while providing a number of new features. OS/2 is more powerful than Windows and is ideally suited for mission-critical applications.

◆ Objects represent traditional desktop tools (example: letters, appointment calendar). Instead of working with the actual files, you work with objects representing these files.

◆ Windows are used to organize icons.

Note: To take advantage of all the OS/2 features, you need a mouse.

OS/2 System-Icon View

Start Here

OS/2 System

Information

Master Help Index

Startup   System Setup   Command Prompts

Games   **Productivity**

Notes

Minimized Window Viewer

Templates

HP DeskJet 500   Drive A   Shredder

Help

Services Options Help

Help for Productivity Folder

Use the **Productivity** folder to select programs that can assist you in editing text and icons, keeping a diary, creating charts and drawings, searching for files or text, displaying system utilization, and using a terminal.

Previous | Search... | Print... | Index

◆ Dragging and dropping objects is used to perform tasks such as deleting and printing files (example: dragging and dropping a document into the printer object produces a printout).

◆ On-line help is available at any time while using OS/2. You can also ask for help by pressing **F1**.

Note: Windows can be moved, sized, opened and closed as required. This allows each user to set up their own desktop as they prefer.

TIPS

◆ Start with the on-line tutorial and built-in games to become familiar with OS/2 functions.

◆ Make sure you turn on the "undelete" function. Any files you delete by mistake can be recovered when the "undelete" function is on.

INTRODUCTION
MS-DOS
WINDOWS
OS/2

A large number of applications and utilities are included with OS/2, including the "PM Chart" program shown below.

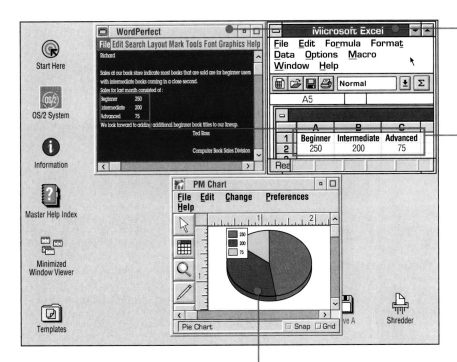

◆ You can also run MS-DOS and Windows applications in addition to OS/2 applications.

◆ Cut and paste allows you to cut (or copy) text or graphics from one application and paste them into another.

◆ OS/2 can work with more than one program at the same time. This is called multitasking.

◆ The consistent "look and feel" among OS/2 applications makes them easier to learn and use. For instance, pull-down menus work the same way in every application.

◆ **D**ynamic **D**ata **E**xchange (**DDE**) enables objects (example: word processing and spreadsheet files) to be linked together. As information changes in one object, it is automatically updated in the linked object.

RECOMMENDATION

◆ OS/2 requires an 80386 microprocessor, at least 6MB of electronic memory, and an 80MB or larger hard drive for best results.

◆ For home use, install your games in one on-line OS/2 folder, and your applications in a different folder.

WORD PROCESSING

What is a Word Processor?

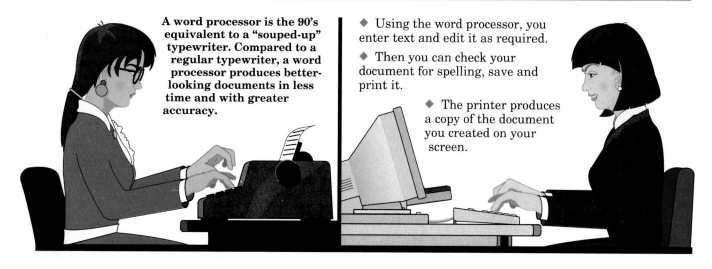

A word processor is the 90's equivalent to a "souped-up" typewriter. Compared to a regular typewriter, a word processor produces better-looking documents in less time and with greater accuracy.

◆ Using the word processor, you enter text and edit it as required.

◆ Then you can check your document for spelling, save and print it.

◆ The printer produces a copy of the document you created on your screen.

What are Word Processors used for?

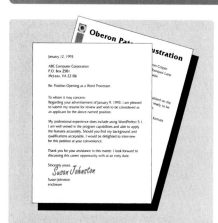

HOME AND BUSINESS LETTERS

Features such as "cut and paste", spell checkers, "undo", and alignment options make word processors easier, faster and more accurate than traditional typewriters.

MAILING LISTS

Documents can be merged with database records (example: a list of names and addresses) to quickly produce personalized letters.

REPORTS, MANUALS

Page numbering, indexing, table of contents, spell checkers, outlining and an abundance of other features make a word processor ideal for longer documents such as reports and manuals.

| GETTING STARTED | THE BASIC COMPUTER | INPUT/ OUTPUT | PROCESSING | STORAGE | PORTABLE COMPUTERS | OPERATING SYSTEMS | APPLICATION SOFTWARE | NETWORKING | GLOSSARY |

WORD PROCESSING
SPREADSHEETS
DATABASES
DESKTOP PUBLISHING

Word Processor Basics

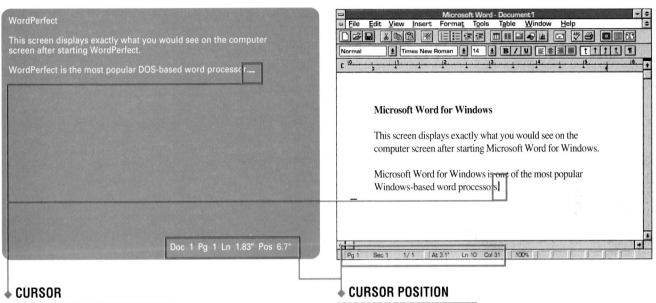

WordPerfect

This screen displays exactly what you would see on the computer screen after starting WordPerfect.

WordPerfect is the most popular DOS-based word processor.

Doc 1 Pg 1 Ln 1.83" Pos 6.7"

Microsoft Word for Windows

This screen displays exactly what you would see on the computer screen after starting Microsoft Word for Windows.

Microsoft Word for Windows is one of the most popular Windows-based word processors

◆ CURSOR

The cursor is the flashing line on your screen. This indicates where the text you type will appear in your document.

◆ CURSOR POSITION

The bottom of the screen indicates the current position of your cursor.

WORD WRAPPING

When typing a document, you do not need to press the **Enter** (or **Return**) key when you reach the end of a line. The word processor will automatically move you to the next line. This is called "word wrapping".

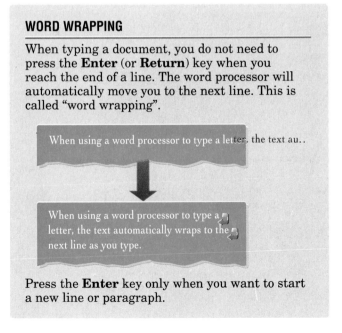

When using a word processor to type a letter, the text au..

When using a word processor to type a letter, the text automatically wraps to the next line as you type.

Press the **Enter** key only when you want to start a new line or paragraph.

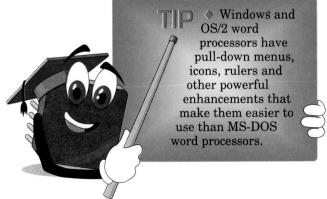

TIP ◆ Windows and OS/2 word processors have pull-down menus, icons, rulers and other powerful enhancements that make them easier to use than MS-DOS word processors.

WORD PROCESSING

ADD OR DELETE TEXT

You can easily add or delete text without using "white-out" or having to retype a letter.

◆ When you add text to your document, the surrounding words automatically move to make room for the new text.

◆ When you delete text, the surrounding words move to fill in the holes left by the removed text.

To whom it *may* concern:
Regarding your advertisement of January 9, 1993, I am pleased to ~~submit~~ *submit* my resume for review and wish to be considered as an ~~good~~ applicant for the above-named position.

UNDO CHANGES

◆ Most word processors can remember the last change, or last few changes you made to your document. If you accidentally erase text, you can reverse this using the "Undo" feature.

SELECT BLOCKS OF TEXT

Blocked text appears highlighted on the screen.

◆ Before performing some tasks, you must select the text you want to work with. For these tasks, the word processor acts on the "blocked text" and ignores the rest of your text.

SEARCH AND REPLACE

◆ Let's say after finishing a long document you realize you incorrectly spelled a client's name throughout (example: Cathy instead of Kathy). A word processor can search through the document and replace all occurrences of the wrong word with the correct one.

COPY

◆ When copying text, you can "paste" an exact copy anywhere in the document. The original text remains in place.

This is the **first** paragraph.

This is the **second** paragraph.

This is the **first** paragraph.

This is the **second** paragraph. This is the **first** paragraph.

MOVE

◆ When moving text, you can "paste" an exact copy anywhere in the document. The original text disappears from your screen.

This is the **first** paragraph.

This is the **second** paragraph.

This is the **second** paragraph. This is the **first** paragraph.

GETTING STARTED	THE BASIC COMPUTER	INPUT/ OUTPUT	PROCESSING	STORAGE	PORTABLE COMPUTERS	OPERATING SYSTEMS	APPLICATION SOFTWARE	NETWORKING	GLOSSARY

WORD PROCESSING
SPREADSHEETS
DATABASES
DESKTOP PUBLISHING

Check a Document

Word processors include many features for checking and improving a document.

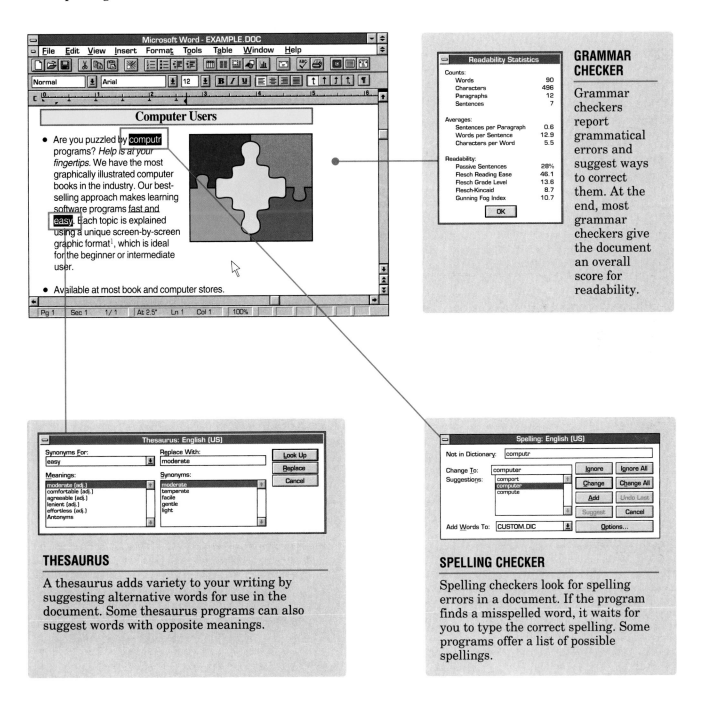

GRAMMAR CHECKER

Grammar checkers report grammatical errors and suggest ways to correct them. At the end, most grammar checkers give the document an overall score for readability.

THESAURUS

A thesaurus adds variety to your writing by suggesting alternative words for use in the document. Some thesaurus programs can also suggest words with opposite meanings.

SPELLING CHECKER

Spelling checkers look for spelling errors in a document. If the program finds a misspelled word, it waits for you to type the correct spelling. Some programs offer a list of possible spellings.

WORD PROCESSING

FONT

A font consists of three elements: **Typeface**, **Type Size** and **Type Style**.

For example, a font can be described as **"Helvetica 10 Point Bold"**. **Helvetica** is the typeface, **10 Point** is the type size, and **Bold** is the type style.

By using different fonts, you can emphasize headings and important information. Fonts can turn a dull and lifeless letter into an attractive, easy-to-read document.

TYPEFACE

Typeface refers to the design of the letters. Helvetica and Times are the most commonly used typefaces.

> Avant Garde
> **Bodoni**
> Courier
> **Helvetica**
> Letter Gothic
> Optima
> Times New Roman

TYPE SIZE

Letters can be made larger or smaller as you prefer.

> 5 point
>
> 10 point
>
> 15 point
>
> 20 point
>
> 25 point

Type size is measured in "points". (There are 72 points per inch.) Most business documents use the 12 point type size.

TYPE STYLE

A type style is a way to enhance text (example: bold).

> **Bold**
> *Italic*
> <u>Underline</u>
> <u>Double underline</u>
> Shadow
> Outline
> ~~Strikeout~~

SUBSCRIPT AND SUPERSCRIPT

Normal^{Superscript}

Superscript slightly raises characters above the line of text.

Normal$_{Subscript}$

Subscript slightly lowers characters below the line of text.

◇ The available typefaces, type sizes, and type styles depend on the application program and printer you use.

Special Features

TABLES

Tables help you organize information into rows and columns. Most word processors automatically create tables when you need them.

VOLUNTEER SCHEDULE	
DAY	**HOURS**
Monday	9:00 – 5:00
Wednesday	9:00 – 5:00
Friday	9:00 – 4:00

INCOME STATEMENT		
	January	**February**
REVENUE	$ 8,700	$ 7,800
TOTAL EXPENSES	$ 7,820	$ 6,560
INCOME	$ 880	$ 1,240

EXPENSES		
Category	**1991**	**1992**
Rent	$ 600.00	$ 684.00
Supplies	$ 342.00	$ 368.00
Advertising	$ 762.00	$ 650.00

GRAPHICS

Graphics are illustrations that can enhance the appearance of your document. Most programs offer a few graphics, but you can also create or pick up additional graphics from other sources (example: clip art).

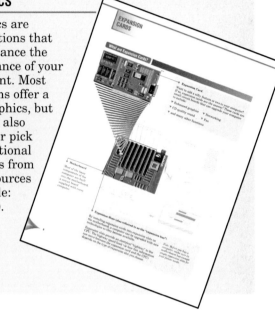

COLUMNS

Some word processing programs can split text into two or more columns.

Brochures and newsletters usually present material in columns.

STYLES

Let's say you are creating a long document and decide that every heading will have the following format: Helvetica 14 point bold. You could go through and apply this format to each heading. To make life easier, some programs let you name a format a "style", then apply this style to whatever text you prefer.

If you later change that style, all headings with that style will automatically change.

WORD PROCESSING

HEADERS AND FOOTERS

A header is information that prints at the top of each page. A footer is information that prints at the bottom of each page.

Headers or footers may include the company name, the date, the page number, or the title of the document.

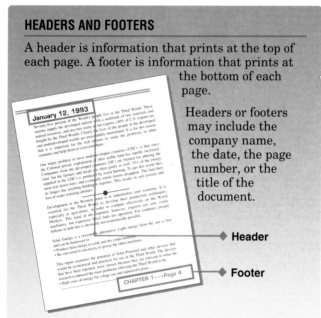

◆ **Header**

◆ **Footer**

FOOTNOTES AND ENDNOTES

Footnotes and endnotes are notes of reference, explanation or comment for items in the document. Footnotes appear at the bottom of each page. Endnotes appear at the end of each chapter or at the end of a publication. Word processors automatically place notes in the location you select.

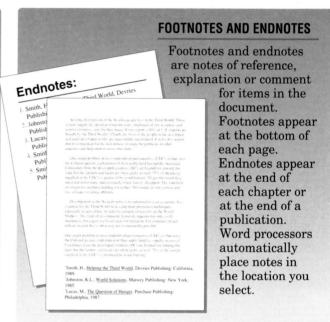

MARGINS

Margins define the distance between the text and the edges of the paper. You can lengthen or shorten the size of a document by changing its margins. Word processors usually set up a one inch margin around the text.

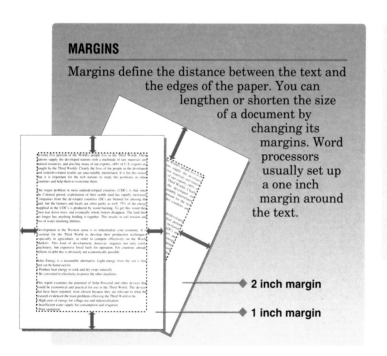

◆ **2 inch margin**

◆ **1 inch margin**

NUMBER PAGES

Word processors can automatically number the pages in a document. You can specify the position of the page numbers on each page.

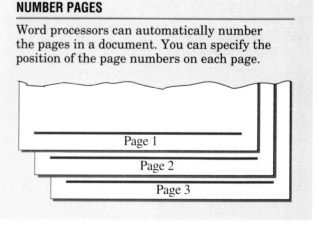

Page 1

Page 2

Page 3

APPLICATION SOFTWARE

WORD PROCESSING
SPREADSHEETS
DATABASES
DESKTOP PUBLISHING

JUSTIFICATION

Left-justified text has a straight left edge and a ragged right edge.

Centered text is centered between
the left and right edges
of the paper.

Right-justified text has a straight right edge
and a ragged left edge.

Fully-justified text has straight left and right edges. Word processing programs justify text by inserting extra spaces between words and characters until all words line up evenly on each side.

LINE SPACING

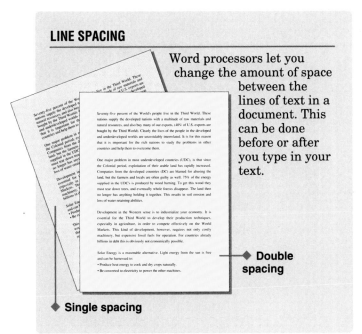

Word processors let you change the amount of space between the lines of text in a document. This can be done before or after you type in your text.

◆ **Double spacing**

◆ **Single spacing**

TABS

WITHOUT TABS					
David Ross	12 Willow Avenue		Los Angeles	CA	90032
Jim Devries	11 Linton Street	Atlanta		GA	30367
Mary Matwey	569 Devon Road		San Diego	CA	92121
Carol Smith		241 Ford Drive	Denver		CO 80207

WITH TABS					
David Ross	12 Willow Avenue	Los Angeles	CA	90032
Jim Devries	11 Linton Street	Atlanta	GA	30367
Mary Matwey	569 Devon Road	San Diego	CA	92121
Carol Smith	241 Ford Drive	Denver	CO	80207

Tabs help you line up columns of information or indent text within a line or paragraph. Tabs in a word processor are very similar to tabs on a typewriter. You can add, delete or move tabs as you desire. However, if you move a tab on a word processor, the text set to that tab position moves along with it.

SPREADSHEETS

What is a Spreadsheet?

Before the electronic spreadsheet, calculations were tedious and time-consuming. If one piece of data changed, all your worksheet calculations had to be redone. With an electronic spreadsheet, the computer does all the calculations for you.

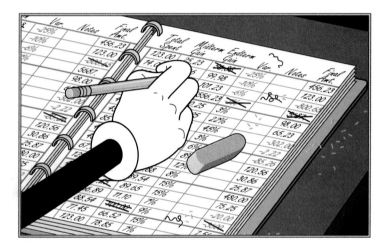

◆ Electronic spreadsheets help you organize data, perform calculations and analyze the results.

◆ Electronic spreadsheets are faster, more efficient and produce less errors than manual worksheets.

◆ Electronic spreadsheets automatically recalculate results when any data changes.

Note: "Spreadsheet" and "worksheet" mean the same thing: a document created with a spreadsheet program.

What are Spreadsheets used for?

FINANCIAL REPORTS

Spreadsheets perform calculations, automatically recalculate results when data changes, and perform "what-if" analysis. Spreadsheets also include formatting and graphing features which make them extremely useful for creating financial reports.

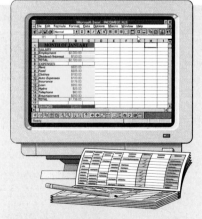

PERSONAL FINANCES

With a spreadsheet, you can track all your personal finances, balance your checkbook, follow your budget, compare investments, and do your taxes.

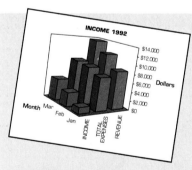

GRAPHS

You can create graphs directly from the spreadsheet data. Graphs help to visually illustrate relationships between different items.

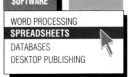

WORD PROCESSING
SPREADSHEETS
DATABASES
DESKTOP PUBLISHING

Spreadsheet Basics

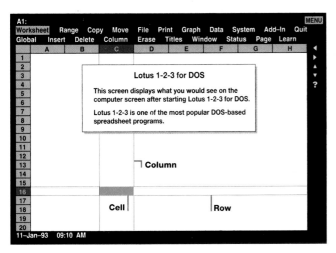

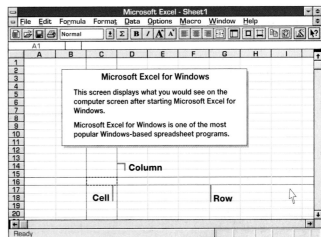

CELL

A cell is a box where you can enter data into your spreadsheet.

ROW

A row is a horizontal line of cells, like a row of plants in a garden.

COLUMN

A column is a vertical line of cells, like a column on a building.

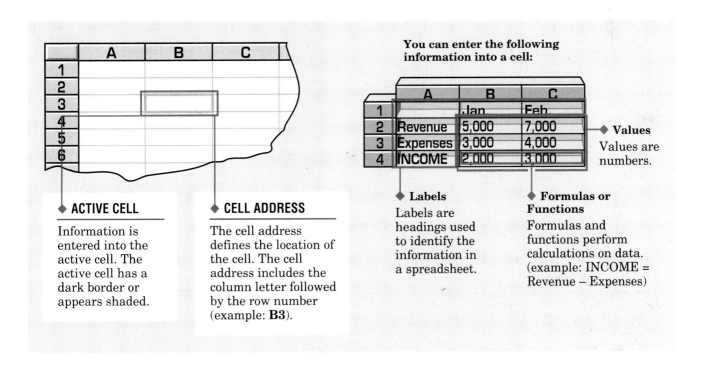

◆ ACTIVE CELL

Information is entered into the active cell. The active cell has a dark border or appears shaded.

◆ CELL ADDRESS

The cell address defines the location of the cell. The cell address includes the column letter followed by the row number (example: **B3**).

You can enter the following information into a cell:

◆ Labels

Labels are headings used to identify the information in a spreadsheet.

◆ Values

Values are numbers.

◆ Formulas or Functions

Formulas and functions perform calculations on data. (example: INCOME = Revenue – Expenses)

SPREADSHEETS

Formulas

Formulas help you analyze data in a worksheet. With a formula you can perform calculations such as adding and multiplying on worksheet values.

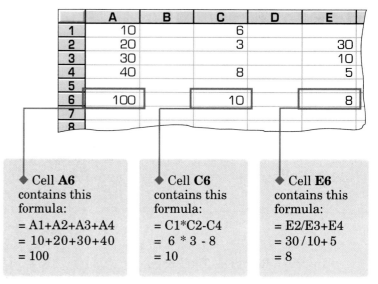

	A	B	C	D	E
1	10		6		
2	20		3		30
3	30				10
4	40		8		5
5					
6	100		10		8
7					
8					

◆ Cell **A6** contains this formula:

= A1+A2+A3+A4
= 10+20+30+40
= 100

◆ Cell **C6** contains this formula:

= C1*C2-C4
= 6 * 3 - 8
= 10

◆ Cell **E6** contains this formula:

= E2/E3+E4
= 30/10+5
= 8

Functions

Functions are formulas built into the spreadsheet program that perform common calculations.

	A	B	C	D	E
1	10		10		10
2	20		20		20
3	30		30		30
4	60		60		60
5					
6	120		30		60
7					
8					

SUM adds together a list of numbers.

◆ Cell **A6** contains this function:

= **SUM**(A1:A4)
= A1+A2+A3+A4
= 10+20+30+60
= 120

AVERAGE obtains the average value of a list of numbers.

◆ Cell **C6** contains this function:

= **AVERAGE**(C1:C4)
= (C1+C2+C3+C4)/4
= (10+20+30+60)/4
= 30

MAXIMUM finds the largest value in a list of numbers.

◆ Cell **E6** contains this function:

= **MAX**(E1:E4).
= 60

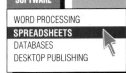

WORD PROCESSING
SPREADSHEETS
DATABASES
DESKTOP PUBLISHING

Automatic Recalculation

If any data changes in a manual spreadsheet, you have to redo all your calculations.

If any data changes in an electronic spreadsheet, the program will automatically recalculate the new results.

	A	B	C	D
1	Revenue		$8,000	
2				
3	Rent		$1,700	
4	Payroll		$1,900	
5	Cost of Goods		$3,800	
6	Total Expenses		$7,400	
7				
8	Income		$600	

$3,500

	A	B	C	D
1	Revenue		$8,000	
2				
3	Rent		$1,700	
4	Payroll		$1,900	
5	Cost of Goods		$3,500	
6	Total Expenses		$7,100	
7				
8	Income		$900	

The spreadsheet above contains two formulas:

◆ Total Expenses = Rent+Payroll+Cost of Goods

◆ Income = Revenue – Total Expenses

If the Cost of Goods value changes, both the Total Expenses and Income formulas will reflect the change.

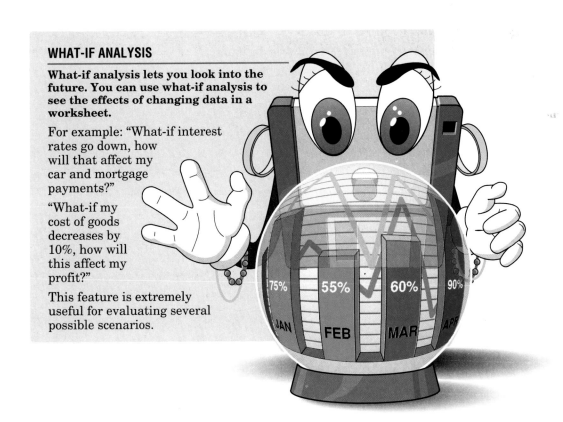

WHAT-IF ANALYSIS

What-if analysis lets you look into the future. You can use what-if analysis to see the effects of changing data in a worksheet.

For example: "What-if interest rates go down, how will that affect my car and mortgage payments?"

"What-if my cost of goods decreases by 10%, how will this affect my profit?"

This feature is extremely useful for evaluating several possible scenarios.

SPREADSHEETS

Format a Spreadsheet

FORMAT NUMBERS

Spreadsheets include a variety of number formats. The format defines how a number looks on the screen, but does not affect the number itself.

After entering data in a worksheet, you can easily change the number format.

Comma	1,000.00
Currency	$1,000.00
Normal	1000.00
Percent	1000.00%
Scientific	1.00E+03

ALIGN TEXT

Data can be left-aligned, right-aligned or centered in a cell.

TEXT	Left-align

TEXT	Right-align

TEXT	Center

FONTS

By using different fonts in a spreadsheet you can emphasize headings and important information.

Note: For more information on fonts, see page 82.

ADD BORDERS AND SHADING

INCOME STATEMENT 1992			
	Jan	Feb	Mar	Year-to-Date
REVENUE	$8,700	$11,500	$13,670	$33,870
Rent	$1,750	$1,750	$1,750	$5,250
Payroll	$1,890	$1,980	$2,030	$5,900
Cost of Goods	$3,850	$4,850	$5,250	$13,950
TOTAL EXPENSES	$7,490	$8,580	$9,030	$25,100
INCOME	$1,210	$2,920	$4,640	$8,770

You can add lines and shading to a spreadsheet to enhance your work.

ADD COLOR

INCOME STATEMENT 1992			
	Jan	Feb	Mar	Year-to-Date
REVENUE	$8,700	$11,500	$13,670	$33,870
Rent	$1,750	$1,750	$1,750	$5,250
Payroll	$1,890	$1,980	$2,030	$5,900
Cost of Goods	$3,850	$4,850	$5,250	$13,950
TOTAL EXPENSES	$7,490	$8,580	$9,030	$25,100
INCOME	$1,210	$2,920	$4,640	$8,770

You can use color to emphasize important data or set apart sections of a worksheet.

WORD PROCESSING
SPREADSHEETS
DATABASES
DESKTOP PUBLISHING

Graphs

CREATE A GRAPH

◆ Graphs allow you to quickly see the outcome of your spreadsheet calculations.

You can easily create a graph directly from your worksheet data. For example: the Chart Wizard feature in Microsoft Excel leads you through five steps to create a graph.

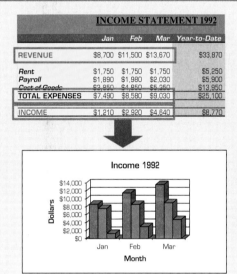

GRAPH TYPES

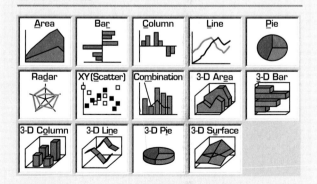

Spreadsheet programs offer many types of graphs to choose from. These range from simple line graphs to three-dimensional graphs.

LEGEND

■ REVENUE
■ TOTAL EXPENSES
■ INCOME

A legend explains the symbols or colors used in a graph. Spreadsheet programs can automatically create a legend from your data.

DATABASES

A database is any collection of information. Common "paper databases" include telephone books, dictionaries, recipe cards, baseball cards and television guides.

An electronic database is any collection of information stored in a computer. Think of your computer as your own personal information "assistant" always ready to store, retrieve, organize and compare records for you.

| GETTING STARTED | THE BASIC COMPUTER | INPUT/ OUTPUT | PROCESSING | STORAGE | PORTABLE COMPUTERS | OPERATING SYSTEMS | APPLICATION SOFTWARE | NETWORKING | GLOSSARY |

WORD PROCESSING
SPREADSHEETS
DATABASES
DESKTOP PUBLISHING

What are Databases used for?

ANALYZE INFORMATION

Which product lines are losing money and should be discontinued? Which employees are better at selling "widgets"? Not sure? You can use the database to assist you in making quick and accurate decisions based on the information stored in your database.

CREATE AND MAINTAIN MAILING LISTS

Information stored in a database can be used to create and maintain mailing lists. Using the "tools" included with the database application, mailings can be targeted to specific groups (example: customers who have purchased over $100 in the past month).

KEEP TRACK OF INFORMATION

Databases can be custom designed to keep track of inventories, payrolls, invoicing or just about any other collection of information. Information can come from one or several sources (example: a network of computers) and can be updated continuously if necessary.

DATABASES

You can use a database to collect, store and organize your information. Once it is stored, you can quickly retrieve any of your data to review or update.

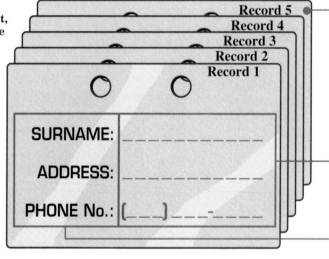

SURNAME: _____

ADDRESS: _____

PHONE No.: (_____) ____-_____

◆ A database file is made up of a collection of "records".

◆ Records are used to group together related facts (example: information on a client).

◆ Each piece of data is stored in a field. Fields can hold information such as names, addresses, telephone numbers and dates.

◆ Each field has a name to distinguish it from other fields.

What Makes up a Field?

Each field has many unique characteristics. These characteristics control how information is entered, displayed, stored and eventually used.

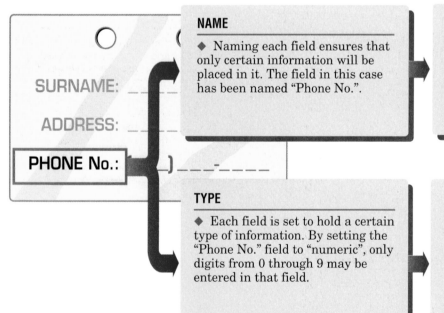

SURNAME: _____

ADDRESS: _____

PHONE No.: _____) ____-_____

NAME

◆ Naming each field ensures that only certain information will be placed in it. The field in this case has been named "Phone No.".

SIZE

◆ To conserve space in the computer, each field is limited in size. You can only type in as many characters as the size of the field allows. The field "Phone No." is restricted to 10 digits.

TYPE

◆ Each field is set to hold a certain type of information. By setting the "Phone No." field to "numeric", only digits from 0 through 9 may be entered in that field.

FORMAT

◆ Information contained in a field can be formatted to make it easier to read.

◆ If you enter "1234567890" into the "Phone No." field, the database automatically formats the number to display as "(123) 456-7890".

GETTING STARTED	THE BASIC COMPUTER	INPUT/ OUTPUT	PROCESSING	STORAGE	PORTABLE COMPUTERS	OPERATING SYSTEMS	APPLICATION SOFTWARE	NETWORKING	GLOSSARY

WORD PROCESSING
SPREADSHEETS
DATABASES
DESKTOP PUBLISHING

Types of Databases

FLAT FILE DATABASE

A flat file database is similar to an index card file. Records contain fields of related information (example: each record holds information on a specific client).

◆ Information contained in one database file cannot be used in another database file.

◆ Easy to set up and use, flat file databases fulfill many simple requirements, such as storing mailing lists and client records.

◆ Flat file databases can only produce limited reports.

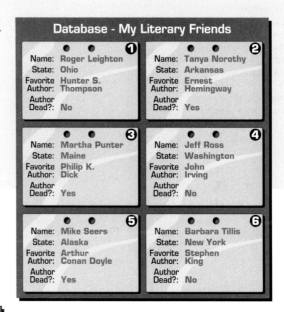

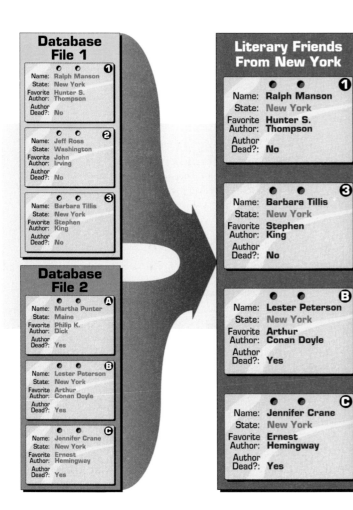

RELATIONAL DATABASE

Powerful, flexible but complicated, relational databases fulfill advanced database requirements. They are often used for accounting and storing detailed company records.

◆ A relational database can take information from two or more database files and combine them into a new file or report.

◆ Relational databases can produce more extensive reports than flat file databases.

In this example, the database searched two database files to find all Literary Friends from New York.

DATABASES

Database applications provide a variety of "tools" for finding and using the information you store in them.

BROWSE

Scanning for information of general interest, known as "browsing", is useful for getting familiar with a database. If the database is very large, "browsing" can be limited to certain records (example: favorite movies of all time).

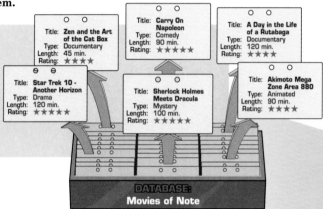

SEARCH

If you know what record(s) you need, you can have the computer "search" for and display them on screen. For instance, you may want to search for all records classified as mystery movies.

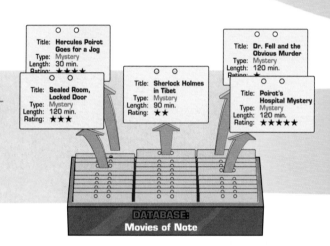

SORT

To keep the database organized, information can be "sorted" into a particular order. For instance, movie titles could be sorted alphabetically.

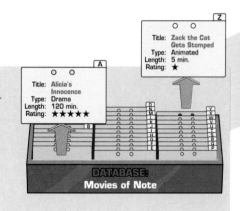

GETTING STARTED	THE BASIC COMPUTER	INPUT/ OUTPUT	PROCESSING	STORAGE	PORTABLE COMPUTERS	OPERATING SYSTEMS	APPLICATION SOFTWARE	NETWORKING	GLOSSARY

WORD PROCESSING
SPREADSHEETS
DATABASES
DESKTOP PUBLISHING

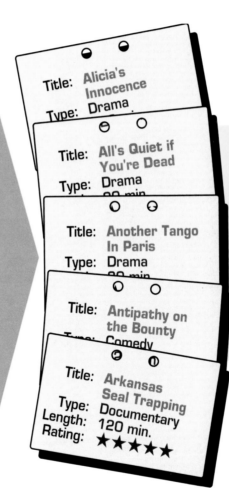

Title: Alicia's Innocence
Type: Drama

Title: All's Quiet if You're Dead
Type: Drama

Title: Another Tango In Paris
Type: Drama

Title: Antipathy on the Bounty
Comedy

Title: Arkansas Seal Trapping
Type: Documentary
Length: 120 min.
Rating: ★★★★★

QUERY

The process of letting the computer know just which records you need is called a "query". A query can be combined and used with the browse, search and sort features. For instance, you could instruct a computer to sort alphabetically and display only those records which have names starting with the letter "A" and a 5-star rating.

CAUTION Purchasing, setting up and maintaining a database can be quite complicated and is best left to a computer expert.

DESKTOP PUBLISHING

Newsletters, brochures, advertisements and other visual documents are created by combining output from word processors, graphics programs and other applications.

The desktop publishing program's job is to help bring all the elements together, producing a publication which is easy to read, visually entertaining and informative.

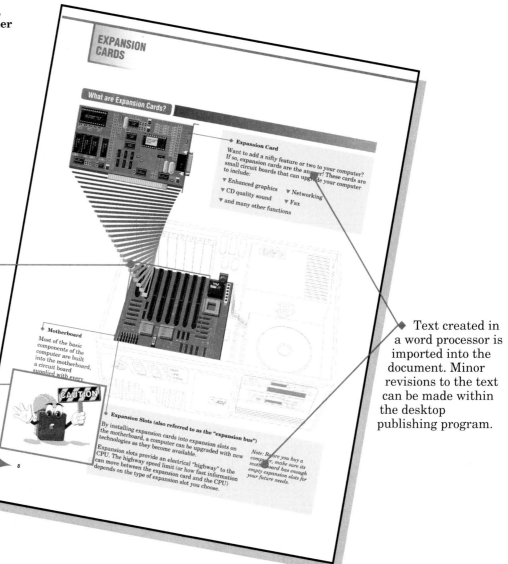

◆ Illustrations are created in a graphics program and then imported into the document.

◆ "Scanned" images can be imported into the document.

◆ Text created in a word processor is imported into the document. Minor revisions to the text can be made within the desktop publishing program.

SERVICE BUREAUS

While most documents can be printed out on the office printer, files requiring high-quality output can be sent to a "service bureau".

Service bureaus use special laser printers known as "imagesetters" to produce high-resolution output. Some service bureaus also offer services such as high-quality scanning and color proofing.

WORD PROCESSING
SPREADSHEETS
DATABASES
DESKTOP PUBLISHING

Desktop Publishing Features

◆ Standard features include moving and sizing images and working with various fonts and numbers of columns.

◆ Most desktop publishing programs can adjust the spacing between characters (called "kerning") and lines (called "leading") to make a document easier to read.

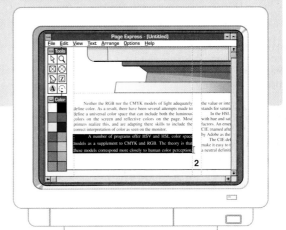

◆ Quality desktop publishing programs include professional features such as the ability to color-separate pages and provide color-trapping.

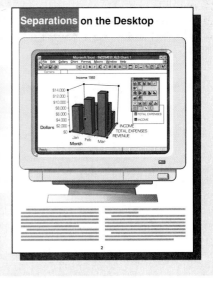

Separations on the Desktop

INTRODUCTION

Introduction to Networks

Networks are groups of computers and peripherals connected together.

A "Local Area Network" (or LAN) covers a small geographic area such as one office or building, while a "Wide Area Network" (or WAN) covers a larger geographic area such as several cities.

◆ Special modems called "net-modems" can be used for temporary connections into the network.

◆ "Twisted pair" (example: telephone lines) or "coaxial" (example: television cable) are the most common ways of connecting computers and peripherals together.

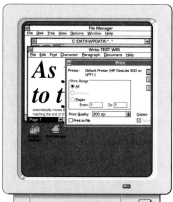

GETTING STARTED	THE BASIC COMPUTER	INPUT/ OUTPUT	PROCESSING	STORAGE	PORTABLE COMPUTERS	OPERATING SYSTEMS	APPLICATION SOFTWARE	NETWORKING	GLOSSARY

INTRODUCTION
COMMON NETWORK TERMS
NETWORK ADDITIONS
BUS
TOKEN-RING
STAR

What are Networks used for?

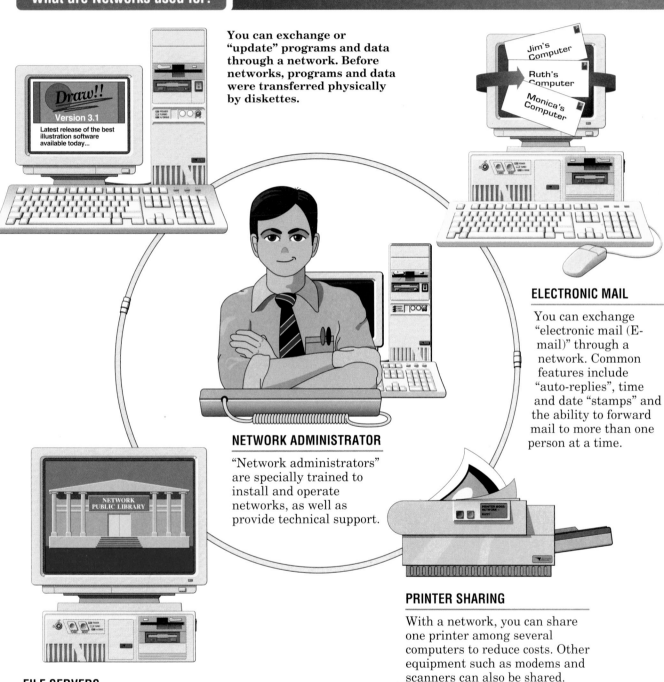

You can exchange or "update" programs and data through a network. Before networks, programs and data were transferred physically by diskettes.

Draw!!
Version 3.1
Latest release of the best illustration software available today...

Jim's Computer
Ruth's Computer
Monica's Computer

ELECTRONIC MAIL

You can exchange "electronic mail (E-mail)" through a network. Common features include "auto-replies", time and date "stamps" and the ability to forward mail to more than one person at a time.

NETWORK ADMINISTRATOR

"Network administrators" are specially trained to install and operate networks, as well as provide technical support.

PRINTER SHARING

With a network, you can share one printer among several computers to reduce costs. Other equipment such as modems and scanners can also be shared.

FILE SERVERS

NETWORK PUBLIC LIBRARY

"File servers" manage shared files just as libraries manage shared books. Passwords and other security measures ensure that only authorized personnel have access to files stored on a file server.

COMMON NETWORK TERMS

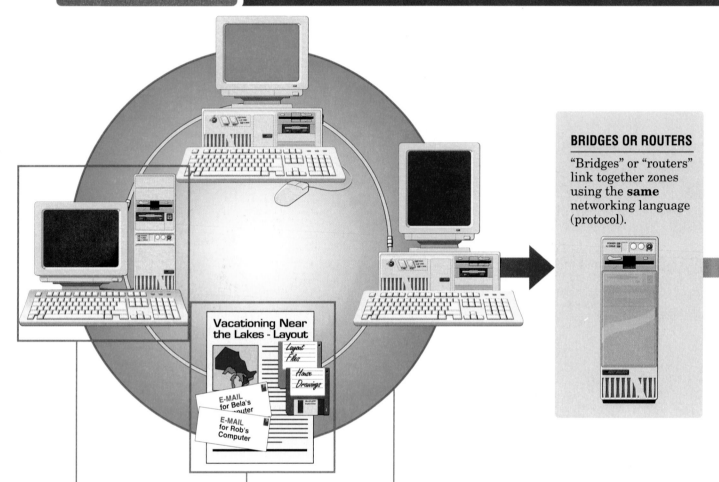

BRIDGES OR ROUTERS

"Bridges" or "routers" link together zones using the **same** networking language (protocol).

NODES OR POINTS

A "node" or "point" is a single computer or peripheral in a network. A single computer may also be called a "workstation".

NETWORK TRAFFIC

"Network traffic" is the data (example: E-mail) being sent through the network.

ZONES

"Zones" are used to break up a large network into smaller, less crowded groups.

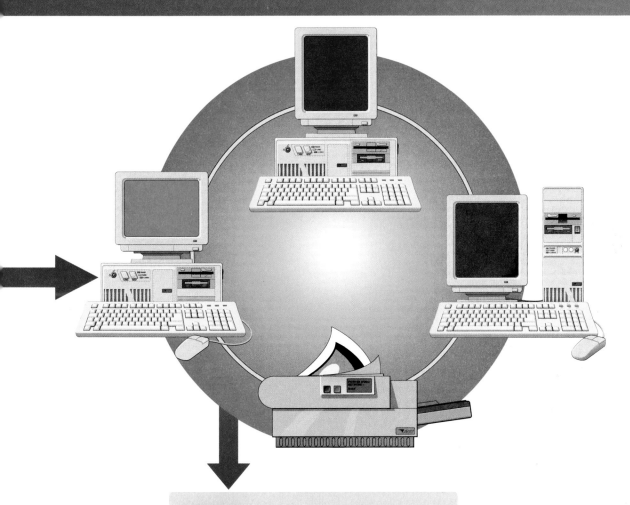

GATEWAYS

"Gateways" link together zones using **different** networking languages (protocols).

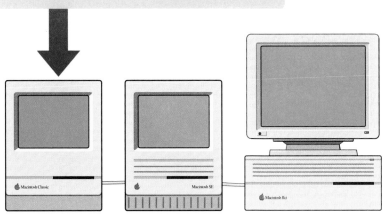

Adding a Computer to the Network

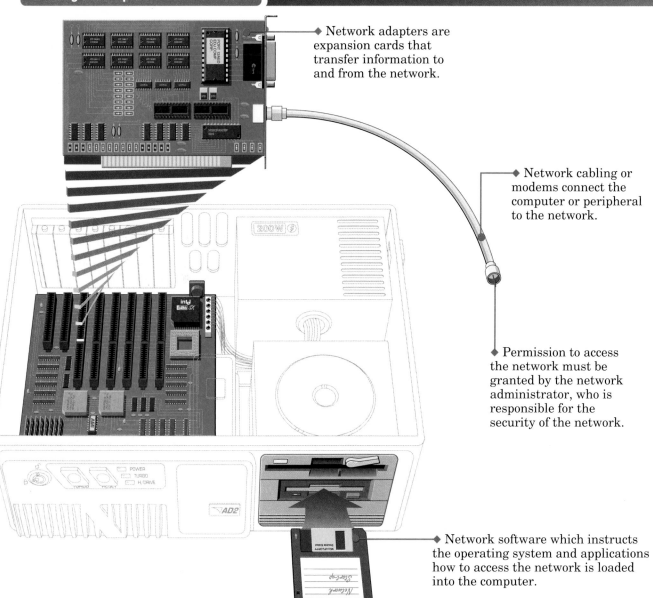

◆ Network adapters are expansion cards that transfer information to and from the network.

◆ Network cabling or modems connect the computer or peripheral to the network.

◆ Permission to access the network must be granted by the network administrator, who is responsible for the security of the network.

◆ Network software which instructs the operating system and applications how to access the network is loaded into the computer.

Computer hardware and software upgrades, cabling and installation into the network should only be performed by the network administrator.

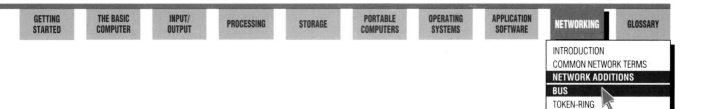

| GETTING STARTED | THE BASIC COMPUTER | INPUT/ OUTPUT | PROCESSING | STORAGE | PORTABLE COMPUTERS | OPERATING SYSTEMS | APPLICATION SOFTWARE | NETWORKING | GLOSSARY |

Bus Network

In a bus network, computers and peripherals are connected to a single cable known as the "bus".

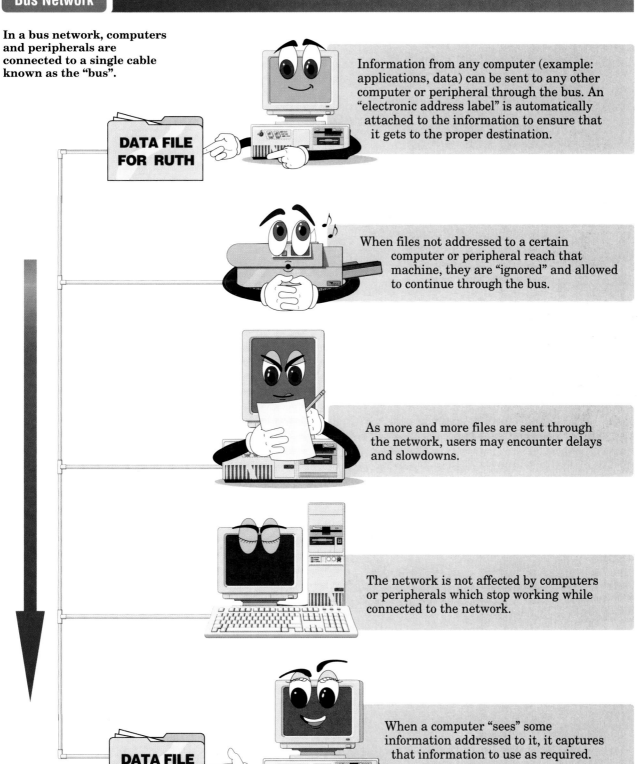

Information from any computer (example: applications, data) can be sent to any other computer or peripheral through the bus. An "electronic address label" is automatically attached to the information to ensure that it gets to the proper destination.

When files not addressed to a certain computer or peripheral reach that machine, they are "ignored" and allowed to continue through the bus.

As more and more files are sent through the network, users may encounter delays and slowdowns.

The network is not affected by computers or peripherals which stop working while connected to the network.

When a computer "sees" some information addressed to it, it captures that information to use as required.

Token-Ring Network

In a token-ring network, computers and peripherals are attached to a cable connected in a loop (ring).

◆ A single "token" passes around the ring. The token is like a "bus token", allowing programs and data to ride for free!

◆ To transmit information to another computer or peripheral, the token is removed from the ring and a file is attached.

◆ Upon reaching its destination, the file is removed from the ring. The token is sent back into the ring until it is required again.

◆ When the token has a file attached to it, it is marked busy.

◆ If another computer transfers a large file, all other users must wait to access the network.

| GETTING STARTED | THE BASIC COMPUTER | INPUT/ OUTPUT | PROCESSING | STORAGE | PORTABLE COMPUTERS | OPERATING SYSTEMS | APPLICATION SOFTWARE | NETWORKING | GLOSSARY |

INTRODUCTION
COMMON NETWORK TERMS
NETWORK ADDITIONS
BUS
TOKEN-RING
STAR

Star Network

In a star network, computers and peripherals connect to one of two devices:

◆ The "central computer" directs files, stores files, and provides security for each user.

◆ A "router" or "star controller" can only direct files.

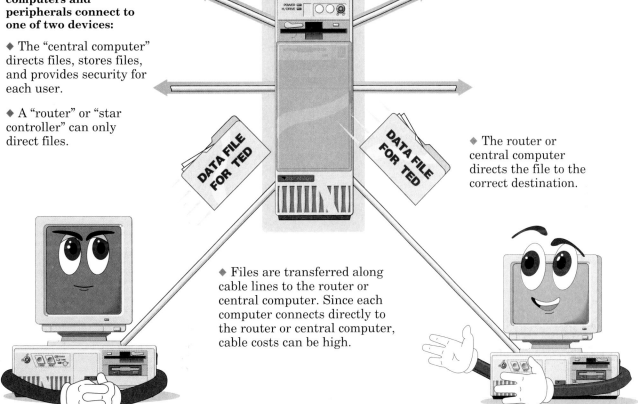

◆ The router or central computer directs the file to the correct destination.

◆ Files are transferred along cable lines to the router or central computer. Since each computer connects directly to the router or central computer, cable costs can be high.

COMPARING NETWORKS

Bus networks
◆ Simple to set up.
◆ Computers and peripherals can be attached or removed without affecting the rest of the network.
◆ Most bus networks allow more than one file to be transferred at the same time.
◆ Failure of a computer or peripheral has no effect on the rest of the network.

Token-Ring networks
◆ More difficult and expensive to set up than a bus network.
◆ As token-ring networks are "closed", it can be more difficult to add new computers or peripherals to the network.
◆ Only one computer can use the network at a time.
◆ If there is a break in the cabling, the entire network will go down.
◆ Token-ring networks are faster than bus networks and can cover greater distances.

Star networks
◆ Difficult and expensive to set up, star networks are seldom used for connecting personal computers together.
◆ Adding a new computer or peripheral to the network is expensive and time-consuming.
◆ More than one user can access the network at the same time.
◆ Since all information is passed through a central computer or router, failure of this unit brings the entire network down.
◆ Primarily used when security of a network is required.

8088, 80286 – Early generations of microprocessors now considered obsolete.

80386 – The third generation of microprocessors. The 80386 is more powerful than the 80286.

80486 – The fourth generation of microprocessors. The 80486 is more powerful than the 80386.

80586 – See Pentium.

A

ALT – The Alternate key.

Application – A computer program designed to get a specific task done. For example, a word processor application is used to write letters.

B

Backup – (v) to make a duplicate copy of data in case the original is lost or damaged.

　　(n) duplicate copy.

Bit – The smallest unit of information in a computer system. Bit is short for binary digit; either a "1" or a "0".

Board – A cluster of electronic chips and circuitry used to operate or enhance a computer. Different boards perform different functions.

Boot – The process of turning the computer on. The computer has a "bootstrap routine" that tells the hardware what to do when the power comes on.

BPS – Bits Per Second. The speed at which data is transmitted.

Bridge – The links between zones of a network. The zones must all use the same language (protocol).

Buffer – The space reserved in a computer or printer's memory (RAM) for temporarily storing data.

Bus – A set of wires or conductors carrying signals between parts of a computer system or between parts of a network.

Bus network – A group of computers and peripherals connected by a single cable.

Byte – One character of information. A byte is made up of eight bits.

C

Cache – A separate area of memory where the computer stores a copy of frequently used information for quick access. A disk cache uses electronic memory (RAM) to speed the operation of the hard drive. A memory cache uses super-fast electronic memory (SRAM) to increase the processing speed of the computer.

Card – See Expansion card.

CD-ROM – A permanent storage device which uses a laser disk drive to read the information. Stands for Compact Disc-Read Only Memory. It is used to store large quantities of information that do not need to be changed, such as an encyclopedia.

Chip – A small piece of silicon containing thousands or millions of electrical elements. Also called an integrated circuit.

Click – The process of quickly pressing and releasing a mouse button.

Clone – An imitation. Generally used to mean any computer that is not an IBM but acts like one.

Compatible – See Clone.

Compression – A means of storing or transmitting data by eliminating redundant information. It allows the same amount of data to be stored in a smaller space.

Conventional memory – The first 640K of electronic memory in a computer used to run the operating system and applications.

CPS – Characters Per Second.

CPU – The main computer chip that interprets and executes instructions. CPU is short for Central Processing Unit.

CTRL – The Control key.

Cursor – The point on a computer's monitor that indicates a point of action or attention. Usually appears as a flashing line.

Cursor keys – The keys on a computer keyboard marked with arrows, used to move the cursor around the screen.

D

Default – The predetermined action taken when no other choice is made.

Desktop case – The style of computer case that sits on top of the desk.

DIP switch – A small box containing tiny switches. Various options are set according to the positions of these switches.

Diskette – A small, flexible disk used to store information or programs. The newer ones are encased in a hard plastic cover, but the disk inside is still flexible.

MicroFLOPPY Double Sided

Docking station – A device that allows a portable computer to be attached ("docked") to a desktop computer. The docking station allows the portable computer to use the resources of the desktop computer. It also recharges the portable computer's battery.

Dot matrix – An impact printer that uses a pattern (matrix) of dots (steel pins) arranged in rows and columns to print text or graphics.

Dot pitch – A measurement of the size of the holes on a monitor screen. The smaller the dot pitch, the finer the resolution.

Double-click – The process of quickly pressing and releasing a mouse button twice.

Double-density – Refers to how much information a disk can hold. Double-density disks hold less information than high-density disks.

Drag and drop – The process of aiming the mouse pointer at an item on the screen, holding down a mouse button and moving your hand to "drag" it to a new location. Releasing the mouse button "drops" the item.

DX – A type of microprocessor. A DX is faster and more powerful than an SX, but slower and less powerful than a DX2.

DX2 – A type of microprocessor. DX2 microprocessors are faster than SL, SX and DX microprocessors.

E

EISA – A fast and expensive type of expansion slot. EISA is short for Enhanced Industry Standard Architecture.

E-mail – Sends messages to another person on a network. E-mail stands for Electronic mail.

Escape – The computer key most often used to mean "oops".

Expansion card (expansion board) – A piece of hardware that plugs into your computer to expand its capabilities.

Expansion slot (expansion bus) – The area on the motherboard of the computer where the expansion card plugs in.

Extended memory – Electronic memory in a computer above 1 megabyte. Most of the newer software can take advantage of this extra memory.

F

Fax – A way of transmitting copies of documents over telephone lines. Fax is short for Facsimile.

File server – The computer on a network that stores programs and data. The file server is available to all computers on the network.

Floppy – Also called floppy disk or diskette. A small, flexible disk used to store information or programs. The newer ones are encased in a hard plastic cover, but the disk inside is still flexible.

Function keys – Keys labelled F1 through F12. They perform special functions, depending on the program you are using.

G

Gas plasma – A type of screen used in portable computers. It is orange in appearance and not suitable for use in sunlight.

Gateway – A device that connects zones of a network which use different languages (protocols).

Gigabyte (GB) – Approximately one billion (or a thousand million) characters.

H

Hard disk – A storage device made up of hard metal platters. Information is stored magnetically on these platters. They operate much faster than floppy disk drives and hold more information.

Hardware – Any physical part of the computer, including the computer case, keyboard and monitor.

Hertz – A unit of frequency that means cycles per second.

High-density – The amount of information a disk can hold. High-density disks hold more information than double-density disks.

I

IDE – A standard used for connecting a hard drive to a computer. IDE hard drives are very common and relatively inexpensive.

Input – Any information you put into the computer.

Intel – The manufacturer of the most popular microprocessors or CPUs.

ISA – A relatively slow, inexpensive type of expansion slot. ISA is short for Industry Standard Architecture.

J

Joystick – A pointing device used in computer games.

K

Kilobyte (K) – Approximately one thousand characters. Actually 2^{10} or 1024 bytes.

L

LAN – A network that covers a small geographic area such as one office or building. LAN stands for Local Area Network.

Laser printer – A printer that uses a laser beam to create an image on paper.

LCD – The screens most commonly used in portable computers. LCD stands for Liquid Crystal Display.

Local bus – A type of expansion slot. Local bus expansion slots operate much faster than EISA and MCA expansion slots.

M

Math Coprocessor – Part of a microprocessor or a companion chip designed to perform complex calculations.

MCA – A fast and expensive type of expansion slot. MCA is short for Micro Channel Architecture.

Megabyte (MB) – Approximately one million characters. Actually 2^{20} or 1,048,576 bytes.

Megahertz (MHz) – A unit of frequency that means one million cycles per second.

Memory – The area where the computer stores the information it is currently working with. It is temporary, so if the computer loses power, all information in memory is lost. Also called RAM.

Microprocessor – A single chip containing all the elements of a computer's central processing unit.

Modem – A device that allows computers to communicate through telephone lines.

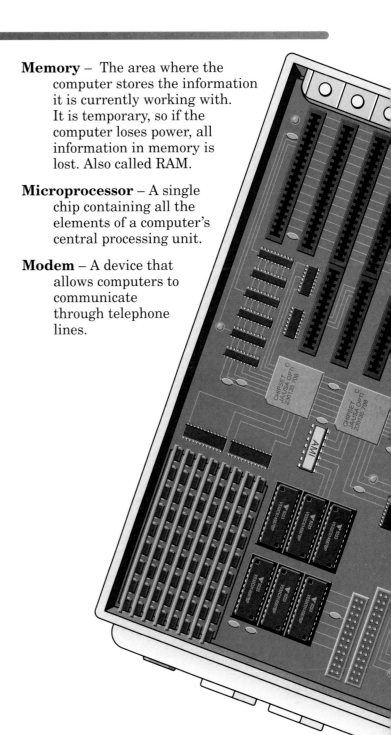

Monitor – A television-like device used for displaying visual output.

Motherboard – The main circuit board of a computer which carries electrical signals to and from various parts of the computer.

Mouse – A hand-held device that is moved on a flat surface to move a cursor on the screen.

MS–DOS – Microsoft Disk Operating System, the most popular operating system for personal computers.

Multimedia – A combination of text, graphics, sound, animation and video that is becoming increasingly popular.

Multitasking – The ability of an operating system to work with several application programs at the same time.

N

Network – Computers that are linked together to share data, programs and peripherals.

Node (point) – A junction of communication paths in a network, usually meaning a workstation on the network.

Notebook – A type of small, portable computer, usually run on batteries.

O

OCR – The process of "reading" text into a computer using a scanner. OCR is short for Optical Character Recognition.

Operating system – The "master control" program that supervises all other programs that run on a computer. It is responsible for interpreting commands, controlling input and output and operating the disk drives.

OS/2 – An operating system for personal computers. See Operating system.

Output – Any information the computer gives back to you.

OverDrive – A chip that increases the computer's performance by up to 70%.

P

Parallel port – An outlet on a computer used to attach a device, such as a printer. A parallel port sends the data (bits) down the wire side by side (parallel to each other).

PC – An electronic device used to perform tasks for a user. PC stands for Personal Computer.

PCMCIA – A type of expansion slot or card commonly used in portable computers. PCMCIA stands for Personal Computer Memory Card International Association.

Pentium – The fifth generation of microprocessors. The Pentium is two to three times faster than the 80486.

Peripheral – Any piece of hardware attached to the outside of a computer. Examples are printers and modems.

Pixel – Short for "picture element". A pixel is the smallest dot the computer can control on the screen.

Point – A measure of type size. One point is 1/72 of an inch.

Portable – A small computer that usually runs on batteries. Portable computers are also called Laptop, Notebook, Sub-notebook and Palmtop.

Protocol – The "language" or set of rules used to communicate between two computers.

R

RAM – The electronic memory of a computer which is used to temporarily hold information. This information is erased as soon as the power is turned off. RAM stands for Random Access Memory.

Resolution – The size and quantity of dots that make up a printed page, screen or scanned image.

S

Scanner – A piece of hardware that translates what it "sees" into a picture that the computer can use. It is like a copier, only it creates a file instead of a paper copy.

SCSI – A standard used for connecting a hard drive to a computer. SCSI hard drives are for users requiring maximum performance and expansion options. SCSI stands for Small Computer System Interface.

Serial port – An outlet on a computer used to attach a device, such as a modem. A serial port sends the data (bits) down the wire one at a time (in a series).

SIMM – A small expansion card that holds extra memory (RAM) chips to add to your computer. SIMM stands for Single Inline Memory Modules.

SL – A type of microprocessor. SL microprocessors include special features to extend the battery life of portable computers.

Software – Instructions or programs that enable a computer to perform any task.

Star network – A layout for a network in which each computer and peripheral is individually attached to a central computer, router or star controller.

Storage device – A piece of hardware that permanently stores information. Unlike electronic memory, a storage device retains information when the power is turned off.

Surge and spike protector – A device that protects the computer from fluctuations in voltage.

SVGA – A very high resolution video adapter or monitor. SVGA is short for Super Video Graphics Array.

SX – A type of microprocessor. SX is less powerful than a DX or DX2 microprocessor.

T

Tape backup unit – A device used to create copies of information stored in the computer's hard drive.

Token-ring network – A layout for a network in which computers and peripherals are connected by a closed loop (ring) of cable.

Tower case – The type of computer case that can sit on the floor or a desktop.

Turbo button – A button on some computers that switches between two preset speeds.

U

UPS – A device that provides battery power if the electricity goes off. This enables you to first save the data you are working with before turning the computer off. UPS stands for Uninterruptible Power Supply.

V

VGA – A high resolution video adapter or monitor. VGA stands for Video Graphics Array.

Video adapter – The piece of hardware that controls the monitor. It is built into the computer's motherboard or installed as an expansion card. Common types are VGA and SVGA.

W

WAN – A network that covers a large geographic area such as several cities. WAN stands for Wide Area Network.

Windows – An operating system for personal computers. See Operating system.

Write-protect – A method of preventing the data on a diskette from accidentally being written over. Similar to the tab on a VCR tape that you break off to prevent the tape from being recorded over.

WYSIWYG – Stands for "What You See Is What You Get" (pronounced "wizzy-wig"). Refers to programs that display information on the monitor the same way it will appear when it prints, including fonts and graphics.

Z

ZIF socket – A device designed to hold the microprocessor. It has a release mechanism that allows the microprocessor to be quickly inserted or removed without damage. ZIF stands for Zero Insertion Force.

INDEX

INDEX

Congratulations!

Look on the back cover for more of our simplified guides.

IDG BOOKS WORLDWIDE REGISTRATION CARD

RETURN THIS REGISTRATION CARD FOR FREE CATALOG

Title of this book: Computers Simplified

My overall rating of this book: ❏ Very good [1] ❏ Good [2] ❏ Satisfactory [3] ❏ Fair [4] ❏ Poor [5]

How I first heard about this book:

❏ Found in bookstore; name: [6]

❏ Advertisement: [8]

❏ Word of mouth; heard about book from friend, co-worker, etc.: [10]

❏ Book review: [7]

❏ Catalog: [9]

❏ Other: [11]

What I liked most about this book:

What I would change, add, delete, etc., in future editions of this book:

Other comments:

Number of computer books I purchase in a year: ❏ 1 [12] ❏ 2-5 [13] ❏ 6-10 [14] ❏ More than 10 [15]

I would characterize my computer skills as: ❏ Beginner [16] ❏ Intermediate [17] ❏ Advanced [18] ❏ Professional [19]

I use ❏ DOS [20] ❏ Windows [21] ❏ OS/2 [22] ❏ Unix [23] ❏ Macintosh [24] ❏ Other: [25]_____

(please specify)

I would be interested in new books on the following subjects:
(please check all that apply, and use the spaces provided to identify specific software)

❏ Word processing: [26]

❏ Data bases: [28]

❏ File Utilities: [30]

❏ Networking: [32]

❏ Other: [34]

❏ Spreadsheets: [27]

❏ Desktop publishing: [29]

❏ Money management: [31]

❏ Programming languages: [33]

I use a PC at (please check all that apply): ❏ home [35] ❏ work [36] ❏ school [37] ❏ other: [38] _____

The disks I prefer to use are ❏ 5.25 [39] ❏ 3.5 [40] ❏ other: [41]_____

I have a CD ROM: ❏ yes [42] ❏ no [43]

I plan to buy or upgrade computer hardware this year: ❏ yes [44] ❏ no [45]

I plan to buy or upgrade computer software this year: ❏ yes [46] ❏ no [47]

Name: _____ Business title: [48] _____ Type of Business: [49] _____

Address (❏ home [50] ❏ work [51]/Company name: _____)

Street/Suite# _____

City [52]/State [53]/Zipcode [54]: _____ Country [55] _____

❏ **I liked this book!** You may quote me by name in future
IDG Books Worldwide promotional materials.

My daytime phone number is _____

IDG BOOKS

THE WORLD OF COMPUTER KNOWLEDGE

❏ YES!

Please keep me informed about IDG's World of Computer Knowledge.
Send me the latest IDG Books catalog.